# Valuable

# Valuable

## YOU'RE TOO GOOD TO BE ADDICTED

Joseph McCray

Copyright © 2016 Joseph McCray
All rights reserved.

ISBN: 0991038614
ISBN 13: 9780991038619

# Acknowledgements

I dedicate this book to Shawanda and Goshen. You are the best family. I love you both a thousand times.

To my mom, Josephine Jordan, who made the biggest sacrifice a kid could ever wish for and who left a lifelong impression on me.

To my family and friends, who I believe will be blessed after reading this. Thanks to Richard Bush and Stephanie Mitchell for your skilled editing. Thanks to the countless people who gave me feedback along this journey; your words helped me to shape this book.

To my Pastor Kenneth Robinson and Lady Lenyar Robinson, who continually inspire me to be my best.

Moreover, to those becoming addicted or overcoming addiction to drugs or alcohol, I want you to know that I care very much that you get off this road of addiction and onto the road to recovery and fulfillment in life.

# Contents

Acknowledgements · · · · · · · · · · · · · · · · · v

Introduction · · · · · · · · · · · · · · · · · · · · · ix

Chapter 1   Be Drug-Free · · · · · · · · · · · · · · · · · · · 1

Chapter 2   The Hero · · · · · · · · · · · · · · · · · · · · · 14

Chapter 3   White Powder · · · · · · · · · · · · · · · · · · · 32

Chapter 4   All Those Bottles · · · · · · · · · · · · · · · · · 50

Chapter 5   To the Family and Friends of
            Those Still Using · · · · · · · · · · · · · · · · · 71

Chapter 6   Other Drugs · · · · · · · · · · · · · · · · · · · 80

Chapter 7   Overdose Death Statistics · · · · · · · · · · · · 92

# Introduction

"Valuable," finally found a title that I like! I'm calling this book "Valuable: You're Too Good to be Addicted." I went back and forth about this title. One time I wanted to call it, "So You Want to be Clean," but after talking with a colleague, she reminded me that we don't use the word "clean" in the field of addictions. We call it being drug-free, then I changed the book title to, "So You Want to Be Drug-Free." Then I thought nobody will pick this book up it's all about drugs. So then I was listening to a well-known minister and motivational speaker, Tim Storey, and in his message he said the word "valuable" and it just clicked with me, "Valuable." That's what people are, more valuable than a life of drug addiction and when they come to learn their true value, they will fight with everything that's on the inside of them to remain free of alcohol and drugs.

So, I wrote this book to talk about drug addiction. I am currently a nurse with 22 years in the field of drug addiction treatment. I felt it was my passion to share my experiences and knowledge with the world through this book. I do think that people are more valuable than drug addiction or alcoholism. My challenge is, how am I going to get you, family or friends, to know that a person is valuable? Well, I will tell a story, and it's my hope that the person reading this will buy into my story and later believe in themselves.

My hope is that the individual who is struggling with addiction will begin to believe in the words that are on the pages of this book and begin to take on a life for themselves. Maybe they will go from a life that did not want to change to a life that wants to change. It is my hope that the families and friends of the people that have a drug addiction, this includes alcoholism, will begin to learn more about substance abuse and therefore be more understanding and compassionate and more knowledgeable and start to see the value in their loved one or their friend. That's what you will find in this book. It's about raising awareness. It's about going to another level. All that I know about addiction and even care about is being placed in this book, and it is my hope that you would read the pages and begin to see yourself courageous, strong, and willing to fight this thing called addiction with all your might.

Joseph McCray, BSN, Certified Addictions Registered Nurse

# CHAPTER 1
# Be Drug-Free

How hard could it be just to get drug-free? To the person using drugs, it may be very hard to just get off of drugs. You have tried it time after time and it doesn't seem to work. Well, I got news for you. It does work! Now I'm not saying there is a magical bullet or cure for addiction. You have to pick yourself up. It's not all about willpower. I wish the addict could just say no and that be it. Not quite sure huh, how you let yourself get this way? It just happened over time and you were not paying any attention. You were not always like this. I know you wish you could tell me. There is so much more you can do with yourself. I don't believe you had no aspirations in life. You had aspirations in life, but alcohol and drugs washed them all away. They've got to be playing in your head. There has to be a motivating factor to want a better life; a life where you fulfill your dreams and make something of yourself. I really do believe you want to be drug-free. So would you continue to read, because yes, this book was written for you.

Now, let me have a conversation with the person who has tried to be drug-free or who has had some time drug-free. Everybody wants to be drug-free, or at least to talk about when they were drug-free, or how long they've been drug-free. Being drug-free is vital, when you think about it. It took a lot for you to get to this place. Do you know when you decided to get drug-free? Was it hot outside, or was it a freezing day? Were you at the point when you said enough was enough? What was your motivating factor to get drug-free? Those are some good questions, but you may not be able to recall what you were doing when you decided to get drug-free. Is it surprising to you when you see all your friends talk about their drug-free time and parade all their keychains showing how they have one day drug-free or thirty days drug-free? Don't you like seeing them celebrate? I believe you really do desire to be a part of the celebrations. Being drug-free must feel good, knowing that you finally beat this thing. You finally got that "monkey off your back." Now, what do you do, now that you are drug-free? Do you bask in your newfound freedom of breaking away from the bonds that kept your life searching, but never discovering, knocking at the door but no one answering, seeking but never finding? Now go out and shout to the rooftops that you are drug-free and no longer bound to a drug or alcohol. Many will celebrate with you. You will not be alone.

To the family and friends of alcoholics (current language - person with an alcohol use disorder) and drug users (current language -person with a substance use disorder), It has always been amazing to me how some people are so bold and able to share, "I'm free from drugs." I think it is a good thing to be able to share that news. How come they are not apprehensive about sharing with other folks? Other groups of society overcome challenges and obstacles and are not so proud as to talk so freely about their victories. Somehow, getting off drugs or alcohol gives folks the liberty to boldly share. I think we can learn something from them. We can learn from their ability to discuss their years drug-free and how much work it took for them to get to that place. I know much of their success is due to you hanging in there with them and not giving up on them. You should take a bow at this time. While, you did the best you could to help them, sometimes they fell, and you might be scratching your head asking how come they can't just stop. This book is for you too.

*Drug-free* is a term that is not going away anytime soon. It's something people who have been addicted to alcohol or drugs use to describe the time they have gone without alcohol or drugs. You noticed I separated the two, alcohol and drugs. Alcohol is a drug. It is. One of the definitions of a drug in *Merriam Webster's Dictionary* is something, often an illegal substance, that causes addiction, habituation, or a marked change in consciousness.[1] While drinking alcohol is not against the law, it does cause addiction, and it changes your consciousness or your way of thinking.

## Addiction

*Addiction* is defined as the compulsive need for and use of a habit-forming substance (such as Heroin, nicotine, or alcohol) characterized by tolerance and by well-defined physiological symptoms upon withdrawal; broadly: persistent compulsive use of a substance known by the user to be harmful.[2]

## Compulsive
*Compulsive* here means a desire that is too strong to resist. It is impossible to stop or control not having the drug or drink. It might be the first thing you do in the morning or before you go to bed, but remember, you have a strong desire to have this drink or drug.[3]

## Habituation
*Habituation* means it is habit forming, and if you were to remove the substance, your body would have withdrawals.[4] It would feel uncomfortable without it.

## Tolerance
*Tolerance* means you need to use more of the drink or drug to get the same experience you once had or when you drink the amount or use the same amount of drugs you get no high. For example, if you were a person who drank 12 beers a day and you continued drinking 12 beers daily, then one day you did not get the same high from the 12 beers and you needed to drink 15 beers. This would mean you have developed tolerance.[5]

## Physiological (Phys-i-o-log-i-cal) Symptoms

This means that the person feels discomfort in the body. [6] This is directly related to not having the alcohol or drug available in the brain. Inside of the body of that person they may have tremors, flu-like symptoms, seizures and even death from withdrawals from alcohol or certain types of drugs.

There's a lot said in the definition of addiction, so let's just do a recap.

Addiction:

1. A strong desire to use the substance.
2. It becomes a habit because the person enjoys it.
3. They use so much of it that the brain gets used to it and the person has to keep using more.
4. There are discomforts when the substance is taken away or not used. This will warrant medical attention to reduce the withdrawals. These discomforts can be treated through a doctor's office or in some cases hospitalizations, especially when it comes to alcohol withdrawals.
5. The desire is so strong to use that the person will use knowing that the substance is harmful to them or others around them including children.

When you have an addiction, you almost begin to believe that the drug or alcohol is a real person. You might think this is a person with a personality. Or you might believe this is a person with feelings and thoughts like real people. You might even see alcohol or drugs as an individual who has an interest in another human being. Don't get it twisted—drugs or alcohol is not a person, but what it does for someone may make that person feel like they could never have a friend who is so faithful and could make them feel so good.

So leaving that friend is going to be a challenge for a person deciding to stop drinking or drugging. In their mind, it will be like telling a friend that the friendship is over and convincing themselves that life will be better without that friend. The challenge is, what if that person has been using alcohol or drugs so long that this is the one relationship that has endured, after all the other friendships have died? This friendship seemed to be a bond that would never end. How does a person say goodbye to a friendship like that? Well, I can't answer that question in the first chapter—you will have to read along to get the answers, one page at a time.

Addiction is considered cunning, baffling, and insidious, some might say powerful, around the twelve-step alcohol/drug community.

Addiction is *Cunning* because it doesn't tell you all the failures, disappointments, losses, and shortcoming that are going to come into your life. The drug or alcohol is only going to keep giving you a heightened level of pleasure that will make you go back to it. How could this be wrong?

*Baffling* because you will not be able to wrap your head around what has happened in your life. How did you let yourself get this way? You will be baffled by the money and the time you spent pursuing and indulging in the addiction to drugs or alcohol. You will say, "What was I thinking?"

*Insidious* as it sneaks up on you before you know it. So much will happen so fast, and you think that you've got a handle on things, but before you know it, life will be falling apart right before your eyes. You will wonder and plan to just stop, but you have changed the natural chemistry in your brain, so that when you want to stop, your brain will crave or cause withdrawals that will tempt you to go back to the drug or alcohol.[7]

Lastly, we call addiction powerful. Addiction is *Powerful* because a large number of people who claimed to be strong fell to the temptations. Honest, loving, intelligent, insightful people found themselves slaves to the dictates of what a drug or alcohol wanted from their lives. So many dangerous places it led them. So many shady people they had to deal with just to get the substance. So many lies and games they had to play because their heads were all messed up because the wiring system had become tangled from the drugs and alcohol they introduced to it.

Getting off of drugs or alcohol is work. Some say the person has to want to stop. I disagree slightly. Sometimes they might not want to stop, but the consequences have made them think about quitting. You may ask what these effects are that would make someone stop drugging or drinking. If drinking and drugging feel so good, how could they be so wrong? There was a song by Luther Ingram in 1972 which goes like this: "If loving you is wrong, I don't want to be right."[8] That's what some people who use drugs say—if using drugs is so wrong, they don't want to be right. They say, fire me; take my children away; send me to jail; let my health fail; let my spouse leave me. I don't care. I like alcohol or this drug so much. They don't directly say that, but with the way the drug or alcohol takes priority in their lives, it begins to say that to them. I have heard it said, first you have the drug or alcohol—you have control—but as time goes on, the drug has you, controls you.

I don't think anything has the right to change your mind without your full knowledge of the short-term or long-term consequences you might be facing. Think about it for a moment. When a person is under the influence of alcohol or drugs, they go through a mental change. They have allowed a substance to temporarily take over the normal functions of the brain. This person is going to get more pleasure, more fun, and more enjoyment out of life for that moment. The things that seemed to be weighing them down are going to get a little lighter. The person is not entirely sure of what experience they might have, but they are hoping for a good one. They will take the chance with the hopes that they will go to a place they have never traveled to before in their mind. I always say when people drink alcohol or use drugs, they are not looking for that drug or alcohol to do something just physically, but they want the drug or alcohol to change their minds. Forget about the saying "A mind is a terrible thing to waste."[9] Their saying has become "A mind is an enjoyable thing to waste."

I describe this experience this way: think of your brain as a door that opens a few inches, just a crack. This is the measure of what you might experience from your favorite food, sex, watching a movie, or laughing with some friends. Now think of that same door opening a foot wide because of the introduction of drugs or alcohol to your brain. Now, this door of pleasure was never supposed to open that wide, but you allowed drugs and alcohol to trick the brain to open wider. Drugs and alcohol have the ability to make the pleasure center of your brain open a foot wide.[7] When the pleasure center opens that wide, it becomes hard to find food, sex, a movie, or laughing with friends to compare to the joy that drugs or alcohol gave your brain. Some people spend a lifetime trying to get that door to open wide and give them that first high experience, but to no avail—they can never experience it, because the door was open to its widest point, there is no point more extensive it can open to.

You have heard the saying that the addict is always chasing the first high. They are chasing that first time the door of pleasure was opened very broadly. The longer you refrain from drugs or alcohol, the better chance you have for that door to close.[7] The brain cannot handle so much pleasure, and you are faced with the challenge of getting back to when you had real pleasure in your favorite dish, enjoyed sex or a good movie, laughing with friends. This learning to get pleasure out of things that once brought that pleasure is a lifelong journey for the person with addiction. Having to find enjoyment in the simple things in life. Knowing that nothing will compare with the pleasure you are accustomed to. But now you have to allow your brain chemistry to heal after it has been disturbed all those years you were in addiction to alcohol and drugs.[7]

What about the brain before alcohol or a drug was introduced to it? During the teenage years, rapid growth of the brain is taking place.[10] Why would you want to experiment with drugs or alcohol? The brain of the youth is developing. It's getting ready to be an adult. Why would you want anything to interfere with that development process? Unfortunately, it happens—you hear stories all the time about how people in addiction started when they were just teenagers. If that was you, that's a problem; because your brain was getting you ready to be responsible. It was getting you ready to take on the world. You were to be our next great leader, the person who was to make a difference in society, but drugs or alcohol came along and slowed down that process. They derailed you and distracted you, got you off focus, and by the time you realized you'd been distracted, it was too late.

It is not uncommon to talk with adults who started drinking and using drugs who say, "I started drinking when I was fourteen or fifteen." Those people lost out on a crucial stage in life; just when they were getting prepared to move into adulthood, their maturity went in reverse or just stopped.[10] Some of these people are very impatient, easily upset, and confused about what they want to do in life. Sounds like a teenager to me. These are grown men and women in their thirties, forties, fifties, and sometimes sixties who have not matured properly. They were introduced to alcohol or drugs at an early age and continued to use—if they had stopped while they were young, they would have had a chance to grow up more in their lives. Some good news is that maturity can take place as an adult—returning to where you left off is possible, but it takes patience and time.

Might you be saying, "How come you are writing a book about addiction, and you've never been addicted?" That's a real question. Now let me ask you a question. Do you have to have depression, high blood pressure, or cancer to treat or educate people suffering from those illnesses? You only, in my opinion, have to be knowledgeable and compassionate. Jesus was never a sinner, but he cared about sinners. Jesus ate with them. Jesus healed them. Jesus had compassion for them. He even went as far as the grave for them.

This book is not for those people who have got the knowledge or who know the best plan. *Valuable —You're Too Good to be Addicted,* is for those who want to know more about addiction and for those who want to continue in a life of recovery. I'm writing this book because of my compassion and knowledge as a nurse in the field of addictions for over twenty-two years. I hope that more people become compassionate for people living with addictions to drugs or alcohol. I hope that the individual who is abusing alcohol or drugs will want a better life. Life like the rest of us have. Life drug-free.

# Chapter 1

1. Drug. (2016) *Merriam-Webster.com* Retrieved February 22, 2016, from http://www.merriam-webster.com/dictionary/drug
2. Addiction. (2016) *Merriam-Webster.com* Retrieved February 22, 2016 from http://www.merriam-webster.com/dictionary/addiction
3. Compulsive. (2016) *Merriam-Webster.com* Retrieved February 22, 2016 from http://www.merriam-webster.com/dictionary/compulsive
4. Habituation. (2016) *Merriam-Webster.com* Retrieved February 22, 2016 from http://www.merriam-webster.com/dictionary/habituation
5. Tolerance. (2016) National Institute on Drug Abuse. Retrieved April 30, 2016 from https://www.drugabuse.gov/publications/teaching-packets/neurobiology-drug-addiction/section-iii-action-heroin-morphine/6-definition-tolerance
6. Physiological. (2016) *Oxford Dictionary.com* Retrieved May 2, 2016 from http://www.bing.com/search?q=physiological&src=IE-SearchBox&FORM=IESR02
7. Drugs, Brains, and Behavior: The Science of Addiction. (July 2014). retrieved February 22, 2016 from https://www.drugabuse.gov/publications/drugs-brains-behavior-science-addiction/drug-abuse-addiction
8. Hampton, C. Banks, A and Jackson, R. (1972). If Loving You is Wrong, I Don't Want to Be Right. [Recorded by

L. Ingram] "If Loving You Is Wrong". On Miscellaneous [LP}. North Avalon, Memphis: KoKo (1972)
9. United Negro College Fund. (2016). Retrieved February 22, 2016 from http://uncf.org/
10. Adolescent Brains are Works in Progress. (March 4, 2000). *Nature.com, Volume 404.* Retrieved May 2, 2016 from http://www.pbs.org/wgbh/pages/frontline/shows/teenbrain/work/adolescent.html

# CHAPTER 2

## The Hero

Getting off drugs is work. Take, for example, Heroin; Heroin is great for pain. Wish we could use it as a pain reliever, but there would be those who would keep taking it way after the pain was gone. The euphoria or the high associated with it, some say, is tremendous. Like nothing you have ever experienced.

Heroin makes folks feel good, but in 1924, the United States government banned it.[1] The addiction to it was costing the productivity of the country. Did you know when people no longer produce economically for a country, that country will perish economically? If you look at history, when China in 1799 was using opium, the country was becoming inadequate, as men were no longer producing as workers. The country of China had to ban it.[2] The same was true for America. Not only does a drug like Heroin get you out of the workforce, but it causes you to take what you have earned and give it back to the dealer to buy more.

Heroin was originally given as a medication to help people suffering from pain associated with a cough from Tuberculosis.[3] People named it Heroin because it made them feel like a hero.[3] No matter what we try, we can't seem to get it off our streets because it works so well, despite government rules and laws. There is a group of people who continue to sell and buy Heroin for its euphoric or great feeling. Our government said no, but someone else said yes.

There are some who might say, "What's so wrong with the use of Heroin?" I'm glad you ask. First, while you are feeling euphoric, what else are you doing? For starters, can you go to work? Why would you? Would you be attentive enough to do that job well? You are likely to fall off into a dream state and fail at that job. You could have an accident driving a bus full of kids to school. You could be a nurse drawing up the wrong medicine that could be a fatal injection to your patient, or you could be an officer of the law pulling your gun out too soon or not at all. You could be working at a restaurant fixing food with the worst hygiene imaginable, making everybody sick from the excellent meal you thought you were cooking.

Eventually, even with all your well-thought-out plans to hide your secret addiction to Heroin, someone is going to discover that something is wrong with you. The urine gets collected, and you are out of that job before you know it. That's one reason Heroin is not good for you. I didn't mention how you have to skip out from work to get another shot or dose of Heroin because it doesn't last forever—somewhere around four to six hours is all the high you are going to get—and now you are panicky because the withdrawals are about to kick in.[4] Do you use at work or during your lunch break? Do you sweat through the withdrawals that make you feel like the flu has just landed on you instantly, without fair warning?[5] You've got a dilemma, and it must be solved soon, because of the withdrawals that have gotten to you, along with the cravings to use Heroin. This dilemma must be eating away at you, making you need to use Heroin, despite the cost. Despite the harm, despite the dangerous places you might find yourself, despite the nasty things you might do to get the money to get this Heroin.

My friend, you still want to convince me that you can use and maintain a job? I think not. By contrast, though, I have had a guy tell me that some construction businesses are more accepting of people with a drug habit, including a Heroin addiction. Who knows, maybe they don't do a lot of checking on the background of the workers. He described being "high" most days as he and others built a building in downtown Baltimore. He reports he worked under the influence of drugs. No one tested him for drugs. The rules seem not to be as strict at some construction worksites, according to this fellow. So you might have gotten away so far, but that might not continue to be the case. And there is a safety factor that must be considered for you and the people around when you are under the influence of a drug or alcohol.

The second point is the law you have to break to obtain Heroin. I told you earlier that our country banned it, so to get it, you have to break the law. You have to deal with the whole criminal element of obtaining it or "copping" for it, which means buying or otherwise acquiring drugs.[6] That whole pursuit sometimes is described as a thrill by Heroin addicts. The entire masterful plan of lying, hustling, stealing, manipulating, getting over on people for a few dollars to obtain the funds, then you have to find the best Heroin. To find Heroin, you have to move from your place of comfort to areas that are dangerous. Never knowing who you will be buying from—maybe an officer of the law? Will you be buying from someone who plans to rob you, or will you be buying from someone who told you the Heroin was good? You may find that they lied, and there is no return policy. But despite putting in that much time and energy you can't be worried, because soon you are going to have that thrilling moment, this is the moment you have been waiting for, the euphoria or the great feeling.

 I think this is a most stressful event in the life of a Heroin user. A time of much anxiety and stress. Anxiety is a feeling of worry, nervousness, or unease, typically about an imminent event or something with an uncertain outcome.[7] For the Heroin user, a lot of worries must be on their mind and stresses on their body as they are in pursuit of this substance. Why call it a thrill? I think that's so it can sound like a chase or an adventure of some sort. I would have to say this must be torturous to have to live like this every day.

 Stress is defined as, a state of mental tension and worry caused by problems in life, work, etc.: physical force or pressure.[8] All of us encounter stress. There is no way to avoid it, but we can lessen our stress or reduce it, so it does not take a toll on our health.[8] A Heroin addict or anyone addicted to drugs or alcohol endures incredible amounts of stress. You might be saying, "Why don't they just stop?" Or in the words of Nancy Reagan, "Just say no to drugs."They don't just stop, because they have altered the brain over time by using substances.[9] It will require some work for the Heroin user to get drug-free, some work indeed!

Another concern is the way in which some people use the Heroin; they like to use a needle. If you are the only one using the needle, then you don't have to worry about transmitting any diseases to yourself, but if you share that needle with someone, that's another story. Of course, you may know the person you are about to share your drugs with. You've known them for years, they are "good" as far as you know. But be the first person to use the needle, to get the drug, then share with the next person. You know I am being facetious.

Some people want Heroin to go straight in their veins, which deliver straight to the heart, then to the lungs, then back to the heart, then to the brain.[10] You thought it went straight to the brain? Not so. Now the brain has a chance to feel the substance you have waited for, but meanwhile, who were those people in that "abandominium" or empty house where some users use or sleep, also called shooting galleries?[11] Some of those folks might have had hepatitis C, a chronic liver infection that can be fatal. Thanks to better medications in the past few years Hepatitis C has cure rates of 97–99 %.[12] Or those folks may have had HIV. People with HIV can now live for decades, while under care. It's great that we have great treatments for those once-fatal diseases, but it's still one more health problem that the person will have to endure.

Maybe you mix Heroin with water and cook it to crystals, dissolve, then inject it. Sometimes dirt is within that mix. You inject it into your vein, making it a germ going to your heart. There is no filter in the heart to trap dirt or debris. This dirt or debris then enters your lungs that were waiting to use oxygen. This dirt gets trapped in the heart valves, and we call it endocarditis.[13] *Endo* means "valve," *cardo* means "heart," and *itis* means "inflammation"—some gritty stuff to contend with, because we can never seem to get all the dirt out. Now you may be facing many years of antibiotic therapy, or maybe replacement heart valves.[13]

Unfortunately, sometimes too much of the body gets this "high reward" of Heroin, and you cause yourself an overdose. An overdose is when you have a stronger supply of Heroin or any opioid (o-pee-oy –id) that you mistakenly take to get a significant high or euphoria, but something happens to your breathing. You might think people having an overdose just go to sleep. No, no, no! The brain has been introduced to a substance that stops it from sending a signal to the lungs to work.[14] It's curtains, unless you have on hand something to reverse this process. So all the ice, cold baths, injecting the person with salt water, or ice on the genitals (or "secret place" as my six-year-old son, Goshen, calls it) will not work.

In the past, only ambulance staff had the life-saving remedy, Narcan is the Brand Name or naloxone which is the generic name, but now it is being offered to anyone who is willing to take the training and be certified to administer Narcan or naloxone. The responder sprays Narcan into the person's nose or injects it into their thigh muscle, and an overdose death can be stopped.[15]

Sometimes the person who is overdosing is robbed. What do they care about their personal property when they just got their life saved? I witnessed this myself outside of Northeast Market in East Baltimore in 1988. The person was falling from their feet, and a second person was helping them to the ground shouting "help" while they were emptying the pockets of the person falling! I was wondering, "Why are they going through all their pockets, and why did they run away?" Robbery does happen in some cases.

On another note, if you live in Baltimore and you want to save a person who overdoses or "goes out," you can call the Baltimore City Department of Health and Mental Hygiene at (410) 767 – 6500.[15] Get training and a prescription for the medication to save somebody. If you don't live in Baltimore, check with your local health department in your jurisdiction.

Now I want to talk about Methadone. What is a Heroin addict to do? That was the question in the 1960s, when Heroin abuse was out of control in the main cities in our country. We needed an answer for this problem. It was an epidemic. People were increasingly using Heroin. The crime was on the rise, and overdoses, too. A team of doctors in New York had a goal of trying to help Heroin addicts, so they decided to use an oral medication called Methadone. (Two members of the team were Drs. Vincent P. Dole and Marie E. Nyswander).[16]

Methadone was a pain medication used in Germany.[16] These doctors from New York decided to give it a try. So they offered a study. It was only supposed to be a temporary medication used to help addicts abstain from Heroin. The people in the study received Methadone for twelve months, and then the people were weaned off of it before the twelve months ended. The doctors went back to see how the people were doing, but most of them had relapsed back to Heroin.[16]

The doctors offered a second study of Methadone, and twelve months later, the people had done the same thing again; they went back to Heroin within weeks.[16] The doctors decided at that time that Methadone would be used for long-term treatment of opiate addiction. Heroin is one of the class of drugs called opioids. Methadone was a breakthrough, as it helped reduce crimes, overdose deaths, and needle exchanging, thereby reducing hepatitis C. Methadone gave people the ability to function like normal. Former users were able to work, provide for their families, and avoid incarceration.

Methadone is a long-acting opioid whose effects can last upwards of eighteen hours.[16] It is a daily medication for the treatment of opioid addiction. The first benefit is that the person does not experience cravings to use Heroin or any other opioid or painkillers, such as Percocet, oxycodone, Dilaudid, you name it. If the individual is taking the right dose of Methadone, they will not desire to use an opiate.[17]

Oh, I didn't tell you that opiates are pain relieving medications. They are some of the strongest around. The first ones that came from the opium poppy seed were Opium, Morphine and Codeine.[19] Later we made substitutes or derivatives of these natural pain relievers. Some of those derivatives were Percocet, Dilaudid, Heroin and yes Methadone. We now call them all opioids (o-pee-oyds).[19] Going forward I will refer to opiates as opioids.

Secondly, the opioid user should have decreased withdrawals from opioids, while taking Methadone. People report opioid withdrawals are like going through the flu. The common complaints are body aches, stomach cramps, nausea/vomiting, and chills when stopping the use of opioids like Heroin, Percocet or OxyContin or Oxycodone. You might observe their skin having goosebumps, frequent yawning, running nose, and tearing or crying. These are common withdrawal symptoms in the life of a person who has used opioids. The brain is missing the drug, so there is agitation in the brain.[9] The agitation sets off a flu-like set of signs (what we see) and symptoms (what the user feels). Methadone stops all this by mimicking the Heroin, but not giving the person the high that they would experience from street opioids.[17]

Lastly, Methadone will block the effects of an opioid if they were to use one. Methadone is a deterrent to the user to buy "dope" or Heroin, because they would experience no benefit. Eventually, the user will avoid using Heroin because there is no reward. These are the three things that Methadone did back in the 1960s and continues to do in 2016.

Methadone is one of the most highly regulated medications in our country.[17] It can still be abused, though, because people taking it have found a way to sell it. People who are prescribed Methadone earn what is called a "takehome," where they have the privilege of not having to go to the clinic that day, but rather they can take their dose at home. A person can earn a "takehome" by complying with their treatment plan, such as negative urines, attending groups or meeting with their counselor, but if they are not careful, they can get into addict behavior by selling their medications. Their urine might be negative, and they may be going to their recovery meetings, but they are still operating in addict behavior.

Another reason for takehomes is when a program is closed for the day. The program may be closed on a Saturday or Sunday, so all the patients earn a takehome for the day. Some people may choose to sell the bottle to someone who has decided to abuse Methadone on the streets or maybe is withdrawing from other opioids. Some programs periodically recall bottles from a person in the program to show proof that they are not selling their bottles but are taking their Methadone as prescribed.

I know you are saying, "Why do people look like they are high on Methadone?" The good news is that not all of the people are adding other drugs to their Methadone to get high, but some do. They may take Xanax, a common antianxiety medication. It gives Methadone a boost, and the user feels a greater high when the two are combined.[19] Other pills that are added included clonidine, a medicine which is used for hypertension and anxiety but makes Methadone last longer. Phenergan is a medication for nausea, and it is sometimes added as well. Some of these drugs may show up in urine, but if they don't, the person's appearance tells it all. It is unfortunate, because what was designed to help the opioid addict has now caused an eyesore to the public. It is dangerous to have people nodding and slumped over in the streets of Baltimore, or any city. It happens because programs which prescribe

Methadone may not have the staff to identify impaired persons or sedated persons by assessing them and addressing the reason for the sedation.

A program has to be ready to encounter urine that is positive for any of these substances and contact the doctor who is prescribing them and inform them that they will not prescribe Methadone while the patient is prescribed these other medications. It might take some work, but in the end, the patient is safe, and the stigma behind Methadone is a little less.

As with any medication, there are side effects. The side effects of Methadone can include sweating, constipation, sedation (if the dose is too high), and heart changes when doses are 100 mg or greater. An EKG is ordered at my clinic when patients are approaching 100 mg and performed annually at that dose. The average range for dosing is 60 – 120 mg of Methadone daily.[17] Sometimes this can be higher for people who may be on other medications that may interfere with Methadone, such as individuals with HIV and people with a seizure disorder. There is a myth that Methadone destroys the bones. How do I know it's a myth? There has never been a class action suit filed against Methadone in the four decades of its being in use. I tell the persons who make those statements to go around Methadone clinics and just ask people on Methadone this question: "When did you get your settlement check and how much was it for?" One more point to make. You can get a Calcium blood test to see if you are low on this mineral. This would give you some idea if your bones are being destroyed.

The next myth is that Methadone destroys a person's teeth, again, another myth. I have asked people with addiction how often one should visit a dentist. They answer, "Twice a year." I ask, "Do you go that often?" and no one raises a hand, the room is silent. The simple truth is that tooth decay occurs if you do not brush, floss, and see the dentist every six months. That goes for you and me. I tried skipping the dentist for a couple of years. When I did go, the level of plaque on my teeth was so great that my gums had to be numbed so that the plaque could be scraped off, and I'm supposed to know better.

Are there other treatments for opioid addiction? Yes, there is Suboxone or buprenorphine (bue –preh-nor-feen), or "bupe," as it's called on the streets. Buprenorphine approved in 2002, is what we call opioid replacement therapy. Bupe does the same things for the user of opioids as Methadone. It reduces the cravings to use opioids. It stops the withdrawals that a user experiences, and it blocks the effect of an opioid if a user were to use one.[20]

So you are saying, "Why the bupe?" Well, we needed to treat more people with opioid addiction, and we found a way to do that. We offered private physicians an eight-hour training that would certify them to prescribe Suboxone.[20] By the way, Suboxone is pronounced *sub-ox-own*. Suboxone gave the opioid addict the opportunity to obtain this medication without the stigma of having to go into the inner city, where most Methadone clinics are located, for treatment there.[17] The opioid user could now go to a private doctor and obtain a prescription for Suboxone.[20] Also, while taking the medication, the person could attend Narcotic Anonymous (NA) or Alcoholics Anonymous (AA), church groups, or other support groups to help overcome their addiction.

Suboxone is absorbed best when it is under the tongue, or *sublingual*. Suboxone is distributed as a film preparation, like Listerine breath mints. It is an easier medication to be weaned from, because it does not attach itself to fat cells in the body like Methadone.[20] Suboxone begins to work within minutes, and the effects can last as long as a day. Side effects of Suboxone include, but are not limited to, constipation, headache, increased sweating, tiredness or drowsiness, loss of appetite, nausea, vomiting, abdominal pain, skin rashes, itching, or hives.[20]

There is one more medication we use in the treatment of opioid addiction, and it is called naltrexone, or Revia (in the pill form) and Vivitrol (long-acting injection form); Vivitrol is a monthly injection, and the effect lasts four to six weeks.[21] The injectable form is found to be more efficient, as the pill form has not had good compliance. Naltrexone (*nail-trex-zone*) would block the feeling of an opioid or opioid such as Heroin, Percocet, morphine, or any other if the person were to use one. It does require the opioid-addicted person to be off all opioids for several days before taking the medication. You should check with your doctor before taking naltrexone.[21] Side effects may include cramps, decreased appetite/anorexia, dizziness, vomiting, dry mouth, fatigue, headaches, injection-site reactions (redness/swelling), nausea, stomach pain, and thoughts of harming yourself.

As you can see, there are several medications to assist an opioid-addicted person in getting drug-free. However, some people think that while taking Methadone or Suboxone, a person is not drug-free. I want to say these are our medications, these are not drugs. The way the dictionary defines a drug is as something that can change your consciousness and can be addictive or illegal. A doctor prescribes Methadone and Suboxone. It is not illegal, and it doesn't change your consciousness. Does the person have a dependence on these medicines? Yes, they do—if you take them away, they will feel discomfort. Will they have to be slowly weaned off of them? Yes. Is it a medication that helps the body? Yes, it is. Is it a medication that helps treat opioid addiction? Yes, for the past forty years and counting. Does a person on these medications have a better life than they had before they took Methadone or Suboxone? Yes, if they take it as prescribed and leave out the street additives.

Further, there are some opioid users who have recovered without medications to assist them. I will have to say that the number of people who seek treatment and require no medications to help with their recovery from opioids is small. The vast majority of individuals that I have cared for elected to take medications to help reduce the cravings to use and the withdrawals associated with stopping opioids like Heroin, Percocet or Oxycodone.

Don't let stigmas or what people think hold you up from getting drug-free. I once met a man who had a forty-year history of addiction to Heroin. He never wanted to take Methadone, but one day he decided to take it, and he reported it as being his best recovery after his forty-year addiction to Heroin. When he began to take Methadone, he had eighteen months of negative urine tests. The Methadone worked for him. He was surprised and shocked that he could have such a fulfilled life. His life had been like a roller coaster, up and down, in and out of treatment centers, in and out of incarceration. For the first time, at sixty years old, he now had recovery and he now was drug-free. He realized his life was valuable and that he was too good to be addicted.

Chapter 2

1. Illegal Heroin and United States Law. (2016). Retrieved March 21, 2016 from http://heroin.net/about/illegal-heroin-and-united-states-law/
2. Opium Throughout History (1998). Retrieved March 21, 2016, from http://www.pbs.org/wgbh/pages/frontline/shows/heroin/etc/history.html
3. The Pharmaceutical Company Bayer Coined The Name "Heroin" And Marketed The Drug As A Non-Addictive Cough Medicine. (February 17, 2012). Retrieved March 21, 2016, from http://www.todayifoundout.com/index.php/2012/02/the-pharmaceutical-company-bayer-coined-the-name-heroin-and-marketed-the-drug-as-a-non-addictive-cough-medicine/
4. How long does heroin last? (March 5, 2014). Retrieved March 21, 2016, from http://drug.addictionblog.org/how-long-does-heroin-last/
5. Heroin Facts. (October 2014). Retrieved March 21, 2016, from https://www.drugabuse.gov/publications/drugfacts/heroin
6. Copping. (2016) Urban Dictionary.com Retrieved March 21, 2016 from http://www.urbandictionary.com/define.php?term=Copping
7. Anxiety. (2016). *Oxford Dictionary.com* Retrieved March 21, 2016, from http://www.bing.com/search?q=anxiety+defined&src=IE-TopResult&FORM=IETR02&conversationid

8. Stress. (2016). OxfordDictionary.com Retrieved March 21, 2016 from http://www.bing.com/search?q=stress%20defined&qs=n&form=QBRE&pq=stress%20defined&sc=4-14&sp=-1&sk=&cvid=18559C3707A947DDB6CAC7F274B8120A
9. Drugs, Brains, and Behavior: The Science of Addiction. (July 2014). retrieved February 22, 2016 from https://www.drugabuse.gov/publications/drugs-brains-behavior-science-addiction/drug-abuse-addiction
10. Korpas, D. (2013). Heart Anatomy and Physiology. In *Implantable Cardiac Devices Technology* (pp. 13-18). Springer US.
11. Abandominium. (2016). *Dictionary.com* Retrieved March 21, 2016 from http://dictionary.reference.com/browse/abandominium
12. About Harvoni. (2015). Retrieved March 21, 2016 from http://www.harvoni.com/discover-harvoni/about
13. What is Endocarditis? (October 1, 2010). Retrieved March 21, 2016 from http://www.nhlbi.nih.gov/health/health-topics/topics/endo/
14. How Heroin Kills You. (August 29, 2014). Retrieved March 21, 2016, from http://www.cnn.com/2014/02/04/health/how-heroin-kills/index.html
15. Baltimore City Overdose Prevention and Response Information. (2016). Retrieved March 21, 2016, from http://health.baltimorecity.gov/opioid-overdose/baltimore-city-overdose-prevention-and-response-information

16. Part A: Questions and Answers Regarding the History and Evolution of Methadone Treatment of Opioid Addiction in the United States. Retrieved March 21, 2016 from https://www.drugabuse.gov/sites/default/files/pdf/parta.pdf
17. Methadone. (2013). Retrieved March 21, 2016, from http://www.uatests.com/drug-information/Methadone.php
18. Vogel, M., Knöpfli, B., Schmid, O., Prica, M., Strasser, J., Prieto, L., ... & Dürsteler-MacFarland, K. M. (2013). Treatment or "high": benzodiazepine use in patients on injectable heroin or oral opioids. *Addictive behaviors*, *38*(10), 2477-2484.
19. Hovda, L. R., Brutlag, A. G., Poppenga, R. H., & Peterson, K. L. (2016). Opiates and Opioids. *Blackwell's Five-Minute Veterinary Consult Clinical Companion: Small Animal Toxicology*, 217.
20. Suboxone. (2015). Retrieved March 21, 2016, from http://www.suboxone.com/
21. Vivitrol.(2016). Retrieved March 21, 2016 from http://www.pdrhealth.com/drugs/vivitrol

# CHAPTER 3
# White Powder

'm going to talk about this white powder. I'm not able to say the word, because if I say the word, it will do something to you. I'll just call it white powder. It makes people crazy. It makes a person leave their job for it. Makes another person go out and have sex all night for it.

What's so powerful about it? What would make somebody want to harm or take a life, just to have this experience? You have read the stories about this white substance. No, I'm not talking about sugar. No, I'm not talking about flour. You already know what I'm talking about. If I said the name it might start you craving it, so I will stick to not even saying the name right now.

It's been around for many years. We used it because it gave folks energy. It pumped them up, but was it good for them? Was the brain ever supposed to have all that pleasure that's the thing about this white powder?

Your brain was never meant to have that much enjoyment, never meant to have that much pleasure, but you get it because the powder tricks the brain. It tells the brain, "You open up wide," or it might say, "Why don't you enjoy life more?" It might even say, "Why don't you get such a rush that it is indescribable?" But trust and believe that it talks to the brain and makes it do some strange things.

Yeah, this white powder. People get all mad about it and talk about it, but boy, it sells fast on that street. You ever see them? Man, they are lined up in the alley. First time I ever saw it, I thought it was the craziest thing. It was a cold winter night, folks were standing out in the alley, and these young boys were telling them, "Y'all get up, everybody get in order," and every single man and women got straight in the line as if they were in kindergarten again. It had to be about seventy-five, maybe a hundred people in that alley. I had never seen anything like it. I mean, they were old. They were young. Some of them had canes. Some of them looked like they could barely walk, but they were standing in that alley, attentive, and I said to myself "What are they waiting for?" as I sat on the tub at my mom's home watching. I had the light off because I was afraid that if they saw me looking it might scare them or something, but nothing was going to scare these folks. They were all lined up in that alley. It was so long a line that it went down the other part of the alley, like in an "L" shape. There was a command given, something like "alright" or "line up," and this guy ran through and just grabbed up the money from the people in line, one by one. He was just taking people's money, just taking their money.

There was more; this white powder showed up, and each person who had given him money now was receiving this white powder. After each had received their package, they started dispersing, running in all different directions like roaches. Then I looked backed out in that alley, and there wasn't one soul out there. Those boys had served everybody. They had served this white powder. The people all ran to their little places where they could find a way to get it into their bodies. I thought what a powerful substance it must be, that these folks would stand in the cold, in an alley, over seventy-five people, to get a substance that was going to make them feel good only for a moment, which was all it was going to do. It wasn't going to last to the end of the day. They would have to get back in that alley again, get back in the line again. Listen to those young boys talk to them like they were nobodies.

When I think about it again, they were just waiting for that big moment, just anticipating the moment when they would get that white powder—that white powder that was going to make them feel good for the day, as they say, "just for the day." It wasn't even going to make them feel good for the day. It was going to make them feel good for about half an hour at most. That was all they were going to get. It doesn't matter how they put it in their body. I don't care if they put it in their nose. They could've put it in through their skin. They could've smoked it. Whatever they did with it, it wasn't going to last long. It wasn't going to continue for the course of a movie. It wasn't going to last long enough to watch a television show. It wasn't going to last the time you would spend with your son, your daughter, or your wife. It wasn't even going to last the time you sit down at a dinner table fellowshipping with your family or your close friends. But in the minds of these people, this white powder meant everything. It meant taking the risk of going to jail. It meant taking health risks such as a heart attack or becoming psychotic or losing contact with reality. It meant taking the risk of an infection coming into their body. These people didn't seem to care, not one of them. How many mothers? How many brothers? How many fathers? How many nieces? How many nephews? How many people were going to stand out there and wait in that line for this white powder? Oh, they were going to wait all right. They were going to hold on, no matter how cold it got. No matter how windy it got, they were all going to hang on, and they were going to remain in order, because those young boys who were overseeing it looked like they could hurt somebody. They were scary. They were ruthless-looking even though they looked like kids. They looked like they could be the children of those people in the line. They kept them in order, and not one person stepped out of line. These men and women had their whole lives at risk. Those guys could have harmed them if they had disobeyed. Their lives could've been stopped just that short, just for this white powder. It seemed like they were sacrificing everything, all the places they could have gone and the things they could have been doing, just to get this white powder.

 That was a sight I'll never forget. I never need to see that again. I knew these people weren't trying to get a job standing in that line. They weren't applying for any school in that line. I knew they weren't getting any vouchers or food stamps standing in that line. Every one of them was standing in line to get that white powder, and that white powder was to some of them a cure-all, to make them feel good about life. They had all been fooled. They had all been bamboozled. They had all been mistaken. They had all missed the mark. Every single one of them in that line had missed the mark. They were not doing what they were supposed to be doing. They seemed like they were stuck to that line. They looked like they were drawn to it like a magnet, like bees to honey or like flies on something sweet. They seemed like they couldn't stop themselves, like they were under some mental control, like something had taken hold of their minds. Why would an adult man or woman subject themselves to this white powder? Why would they do that? I scratched my head many times, sitting there on that tub, saying, "Why would they do that?" I couldn't understand it. Why would they take such risk? I still today don't get it.

On the other hand, sometimes drug dealers go about through the neighborhood and give out samples or testers of this white powder. I remember seeing it—the people came running. Like individuals who give out sample cookies or sample meat at the malls, in front of the various restaurants where no one is buying food; they were giving out samples of this white powder and everybody was coming. People were coming from all over the place just running, running, running, running, running over there to get it. You say to yourself, "Can this be a human being doing this?" Is this a person acting so depraved, like they're out of their mind, all for a white powder? I had never heard of anything like this. I had never seen anything like this. All these samples were free—with the idea that the people who took them would come back and get some more.

However, when they came back, they would have to pay for it. This time, they brought money that they had worked for, lied for, or cheated someone to obtain. The money they got by conniving and telling folks that they needed some food or that the baby was crying. They told folks this kind of stuff, just to get some money. You don't think they would tell the truth—why would you think somebody would give them money for telling the truth, knowing well they had no intention of spending that money the way it was supposed to be spent? Come on now. Some of them had gotten this money for little tricks they had done. Little tricks with their body. They had done something "strange for some change." They were there with the money, ready to go, willing to get this white powder. Willing to get this excitement, ready to get this joy. Ah, must've been an incredible joy, to have to go through all that to get this.

For a moment's pleasure, I mean, you did all that? You did all that work? You put out all that energy into getting some money, so you could exchange it for that stuff they call white powder? What were you thinking? Did it mean that much?

Now I will tell you another story and reveal the identity of this white powder. I've been talking like I don't know much about this white powder. Well, I must confess. It was a Friday night, and it was hot, and a buddy and I were hanging out. He says, "Look, I'm going to let you try this white powder, but I need to warn you beforehand, don't you ever do it again." I said to myself, "it can't be all that to it. He said again, "Look, I'm telling you, man. Don't ever try it again." We want to one spot; then we went to another place. Now we were down in the projects of East Baltimore, this was dangerous, man. I had to have been out of my mind. I wanted to try it. What was it like, how would it make me feel? The only way I was going to know was to try it. I roamed around with him. We went and got the money together. He went over to get the package, then we got into a club. The package was all wrapped in aluminum foil. I thought, "That's a strange way to wrap up this white powder." He let me sniff a little, that was all I needed. Oh my God, I sniffed a little bit and man…, let me tell you, when he said not to try it again—"Don't you ever do this again"—I understood now why he said that, because I got so excited. I mean, everything was wonderful. It felt so good. I partied that night and the music was off the chains. I was dancing like a rock star. Man, I danced so much. I got so excited. I took my shirt off and danced even more.

Just then another buddy saw me and grabbed my arm and said, "What are you doing?" I said, "What, man?" He said, "What has gotten into you?" I said, "I tried that white powder, and man, I am feeling good." He dropped his head in shame. He said, "Uh-uh. I'm not going to have this. You cannot do this." I asked, "What's the problem?" He said, "You don't want to do that." He started shouting. "You don't want to mess with Cocaine! It's dangerous. You can get hooked on this and your whole life will be out of control." I said to myself, "How could something be so wrong that feels so good?"

He told me, "You don't want to go down that road; that's why I'm stopping you now. Don't let me ever hear you did this again." I looked him in the face, and he was serious. He was serious. It scared me. I had already been warned earlier that evening, but I had still tried it, and now this was my second warning. I had received enough warnings for me. Cocaine is that white powder. It's a stimulant that gives such an intense euphoria or high feeling, but I needed not to fool with this stuff anymore.

The downside to anything that brings great pleasure is that it doesn't last a long time, and the user is at the mercy of having to use it frequently to get that intense feeling over and over again. Once, in America, we thought it was good to have Cocaine in Coca-Cola.[1] We learned that that was not a good idea. Cocaine was entirely removed from the drink in 1929, because we had discovered it had addictive properties or led to addiction.[2]

Addiction to Cocaine or anything that alters the brain is very concerning. It can lead the person to spend a lot of time trying to obtain it, a lot of time using it, and a lot of money to purchase it.

As you can see, it is a big problem if your time and money are exhausted on Cocaine. How do you have time for work, school, family, or friends? You just don't. Another point to consider is that the Cocaine user who is addicted will use it despite the harm it is causing to him and others. I'll give you some examples of the harm. First, if you're a Cocaine user, you use because you enjoy it, but it's illegal to obtain, so you break the law, and that endangers your freedom. Secondly, you snort, inject, or smoke it, and all these ways you put it in your body are dangerous. Snorting causes damage to your nose—when the Cocaine is in the nose, it causes your blood vessels to become smaller and reduces blood flow in the nose.[3]

That makes for sores in the nasal passageways because of the restricted blood flow. This constriction can lead to holes developing in the nose as tissues there die.[3] As for injecting it, that requires a needle, which is not always sterile or absent from germs like the ones used in a hospital. So your needle has germs on it, then it is placed in your body, and if you share that needle with others, you run the risk of transferring bacteria to other people. Smoking Cocaine, or mostly Crack Cocaine, has risks too. You are placing a heated substance into your lungs. A heated substance burns hairs called cilia in the lungs which are there to help you fend off germs. They cilia are destroyed because of the heat, in the same way a cigarette destroys them.[4]

Now that I have your attention on some of the things that can go wrong when using Cocaine, I want to talk about more health problems associated with Cocaine use.

I said that Cocaine is a stimulant, and it gives the user a rush and a great feeling.[3] That is true, and it's hard to convince the person that something could be wrong with using it—just like I couldn't understand why so many people were against me using it—but I understand why now.

Let's start with the brain. We all know it is the control center of the human body. Everything we do is either automatically controlled by this organ or voluntarily controlled by it. We do some things voluntarily—we have to think about doing them—and some things are involuntarily done for us, like breathing. We don't have to remember to breathe; it's automatically being done all day long. Our heartbeat just beats from the time we are in the womb until the day we are placed in the ground. As for voluntary control, we have control over our emotions, speech, and movements.[5]

Like any drug or alcohol, the organ of the body that Cocaine seeks to influence is the brain. It seeks out our command center. But you wanted that to happen. You wanted to feel like you have superhuman strength. You wanted to feel like you didn't have to worry about life for that twenty or thirty minutes, but like anything, if there is an upside, there must be a downside too.

The downside is that after you've turned the brain to this heightened position and gotten the Cocaine used up, if you don't keep using the Cocaine, your brain comes down, and it comes down hard.[3] The electrical activity comes down so hard that you drop into a depressing, sad, despondent state.[3] You are left with feeling "anhedonia," or lack of pleasure. You had pleasure, but now you lack pleasure. How do you get that pleasure back? You have to find some means to get more money so that you can sustain that great feeling, and this leads to the vicious cycle of addiction.

But I have not finished talking about Cocaine. It does go to the brain to have this great effect, but somewhere in the course of travel, it gets to the heart. Nothing passes by the heart, because the heart is the pump that allows everything that comes into the body to get around on the highway of roads called veins and arteries. The Cocaine is on this highway too. Unfortunately, Cocaine makes those roads smaller, as it squeezes the veins and arteries.[6] This is a problem, because while the heart pumps blood throughout the body, it also needs blood to flow to it. Does that make sense? Cocaine makes the highway, the blood vessels that nourish the heart, narrower.⁶ These are called coronary arteries. What do you think happens to the heart if it is not nourished? I will give you a moment to think about it—time's up! If you thought the heart has a heart attack or, as we call it, a myocardial infarction, you are entirely correct. *Myo* means "muscle," *cardio* means "heart," and *infarction* means "tissue death caused by a lack of oxygen."⁷ The heart did not get its supply of oxygen because Cocaine reduced it by making the blood vessels smaller and reduced the blood which contains oxygen to nourish the heart.⁶ Cocaine is not a good choice for the heart!

This reality came all too soon for one of America's finest basketball talents in the mid-1980s. Len Bias, a star player for the University of Maryland Terrapins, was drafted in the NBA for the Boston Celtics. Just one day after his draft he was found dead in his Maryland dorm room from Cocaine intoxication.⁸ Sadly, the name given to Cocaine during that time in my neighborhood was "Len Bias." I sometimes would hear dealers saying, "got that Len Bias." The drug was named after him to lure prospective buyers. There is an interesting phenomenon that when people die from a substance such as Cocaine or Heroin, somehow those deaths become a way to advertise the product. They give credence to that substance, and people will want to come and purchase it from that particular area where people have died.

We hear the news about famous people dying all the time from overdoses of Cocaine and other drugs, including alcohol, some of them very young and talented. It is a shame! But no matter what you say about Cocaine, it still has an excitement and thrill associated with it. People forget about the risks involved. I always tell people with substance abuse that they have to weigh the benefits versus the risks of the substance. But any user has decided that the benefits outweigh the risks—so much so that they are willing to do whatever it takes to obtain the substance.

Let's take, for instance, Crack Cocaine. There is a difference between Crack Cocaine and powdered Cocaine—Crack Cocaine happens to be the most potent form of Cocaine.[4] It is sold at a much lower price and is smoked. The effect or the high is shorter, somewhere around five to ten minutes, while powdered Cocaine may last fifteen to thirty minutes. Crack Cocaine is so – named because it makes distinct sounds when it is smoked, a sort of popping and crackling. [4]

I remember when Crack Cocaine came into the news in the mid-1980s. I was a teenager at that time. Some young people had gotten drawn into selling it. It was a very popular item in the inner cities, especially Baltimore. It was cheap, and it gave people a tremendous high. What they could not afford with powdered Cocaine they could now afford with Crack Cocaine. The price of Crack Cocaine was around $3 to $5 a vial, versus powdered Cocaine, which was in the price range of $20 a package.

The high people were reporting was extreme. It was so extreme that there were cases where people had murdered family members because they had such a craving to get high from Crack Cocaine. I know this to be true, as one day I went to observe a court case in downtown Baltimore. I would do that from time to time in the early 1990s. I was fascinated with the court process and how as a citizen you had the right to watch a court case. One day I went to view a court proceeding. It was the state prosecuting a young African American male in his twenties who had bludgeoned his grandmother for refusing to give him money to purchase Crack Cocaine. I sat there in the Baltimore City court as the prosecutor displayed the bloody clothes of the defendant's grandmother. He had beaten her to death with a hammer. He did this all because his cravings or intense desire to have Crack Cocaine outweighed his ability to think normally. He weighed the benefits of using over the life of his dear grandmother. The courtroom was filled with hollering and sobbing as this family was being ripped in two from this brutal display of how a grandson had allowed a Crack Cocaine craving to destroy his life, his grandmother's life, and the lives of his family.

I think this was one of the biggest substances next to alcohol to have depreciated some African American communities in Baltimore. I think there were too many young people selling it. They rode around on their scooters going from person to person selling this Crack Cocaine. I remember hearing a story of a young guy selling Crack Cocaine, and the mother in that home had turned her head to the activity. She had ignored the new furniture he had purchased for the home and the new sneakers he was wearing. Interesting—he had no formal job he was showing up for, but he had amassed all this wealth. Where was he getting the money? No questions were asked, and the behavior continued, right in the comfort of this home. This highly addictive substance had come on the scene, and there were those who were profiting from it in a big way.

I once had a discussion with a drug dealer in my neighborhood. He said to me, "Joe, what's so wrong with selling drugs? Really, what is the harm? The people want the drugs, so I might as well give them what they want."

I said to him, "Yes, the people may want to use drugs to feel better, but look at what happens to them. They do not take care of their families because the men have lost their jobs, then the women exploit themselves, and you want to convince me that nothing is wrong with it? From time to time, you go back to the community and give out some food and clothing, like something from the movie *New Jack City*. You have further destroyed your community. It wasn't enough with alcohol, now it's Crack Cocaine. One has to break the law to obtain it. How could you ever give back to that community after you've done more harm than good?"

I said to him, "Take, for a moment, your job as a drug dealer. You are working every day, extensive hours. You always have to worry about what will happen to you. Will you be harmed or killed? You have to be worried about going to jail and think about the product you sold to individuals who had physical and mental downfalls associated with it, such as a heart attacks, strokes, psychosis or intoxication or death.[3] You've just destroyed your community, and now you give them some clothes and some handouts and you think that you've done something good—there's nothing good in that." We could not agree, so we went our separate ways. I went on my way to continue to do drug addiction treatment, and he continued to fuel the drug addiction.

While there is help for a person with a Cocaine addiction, in the life of the person who uses Cocaine, be it powdered Cocaine or Crack Cocaine, they report extreme cravings or a desire to have it. What I hear patients report is that they are always craving or thinking or using. I understand them as saying, "I want to be satisfied."

I heard that we learned about cravings through an experiment done with a rat. The rat was introduced to Crack Cocaine, and then the Crack was taken away.[9] The rat was offered water in its cage, but there was an electrical wire that separated the water from the rat. The rat approached the water, but because of the electricity from the wire, the rat would not drink the water. The same was done with food put on the other side of the electrical cable, and the rat would withdraw from the food because the electric shock was a deterrent. Next, the rat was introduced to the smell of a rat of the opposite sex, and the rat would not want to have sex if it meant being shocked. The experimenters decided to reintroduce Crack Cocaine to the cage, putting it on the other side of the electrical wire. What do you think the rat did? Yes, the rat crossed the wire and was electrically shocked to obtain the Crack Cocaine. The rat was not killed, but it suffered harm to get to the Crack Cocaine. The science world learned something about cravings and addiction. While we are not rats, our brains respond like a rat's in some ways when it comes to drugs.

The question is, what you are willing to do to be satisfied? Will you steal, lie, prostitute, abandon your children, or murder for Cocaine or any substance you are craving? I like to ask a person to rate their craving on a scale from zero to ten. Zero is no cravings at all, and ten is the worst craving. Their answer gives me and the addiction-treatment nurse an idea of how dangerous this situation is and where to direct the patient for help. Sometimes the help is in the form of talking with a counselor on ways to manage cravings, such as journaling or going to a recovery meeting.

Are there medications to help in the treatment of Cocaine addiction? There is no approved medication for the treatment of Cocaine addiction, but Antabuse (generic name disulfiram), which is used for alcoholism, has been used for Cocaine addiction as well.[9] The thinking behind this is that it helps replace dopamine (*dope-a-meen*), a chemical in the brain that plays a role in us having pleasure in life. I have seen it used, and some patients have reported a decrease in cravings for Cocaine, and they have had negative urine results for several months while taking Antabuse.

Whatever you do to get drug-free, it is going to require a lot of work. No time to play, because you will have to work on your recovery with everything you've got. It will not come to you because you desire to be drug-free. It will come to you because, in the back of your mind, you are afraid to use Cocaine again. You are afraid because you are not sure what is going to happen to you if you snort or smoke it again, and you can't take that chance. That is why you want to be drug-free. You like all the others realize you are valuable and that you're too good to be addicted.

Chapter 3

1. Cocaine-Cola. (May 19, 2011). Retrieved March 21, 2016, from http://www.snopes.com/cokelore/Cocaine.asp
2. Does Coca Cola Contain Cocaine? (December 16, 2013). Retrieved March 21, 2016 from http://www.livescience.com/41975-does-coca-cola-contain-Cocaine.html
3. Cocaine. (September 2010). Retrieved March 21, 2016, from https://www.drugabuse.gov/publications/research-reports/Cocaine/what-are-short-term-effects-Cocaine-use
4. What Are the Dangers of Smoking Crack? (2016). Retrieved March 21, 2016, from http://Cocaine.org/Crack-Cocaine/what-are-the-dangers-of-smoking-Crack/
5. Human Brain: Facts, Anatomy & Mapping Project. (March 26, 2015) Retrieved March 21, 2016 from http://www.livescience.com/29365-human-brain.html
6. Kloner, R. A., Hale, S., Alker, K., & Rezkalla, S. (1992). The effects of acute and chronic cocaine use on the heart. *Circulation, 85*(2), 407-419.
7. What Is a Heart Attack? (November 6, 2015). Retrieved February 29, 2016 from http://www.nhlbi.nih.gov/health/health-topics/topics/heartattack/
8. The 20 Greatest Basketball Players to Never Play in the NBA (November 9, 2012). Retrieved February 29, 2016 from

http://www.complex.com/sports/2012/11/the-20-greatest-players-who-never-played-in-the-nba/never-played-in-the-nba-4
9. Anker, J. J., Perry, J. L., Gliddon, L. A., & Carroll, M. E. (2009). Impulsivity predicts the escalation of cocaine self-administration in rats. *Pharmacology Biochemistry and Behavior*, *93*(3), 343-348.
10. Carroll, K. M., Nich, C., Ball, S. A., McCance, E., & Rounsavile, B. J. (1998). Treatment of cocaine and alcohol dependence with psychotherapy and disulfiram. *Addiction*, *93*(5), 713-727.

# CHAPTER 4
## All Those Bottles

I never really understood much about the game of "Tunk," just knew people were very competitive. They would play hours of games, then all of a sudden, bottles would come on the table. They were clear bottles, dark bottles, brown bottles, and tall bottles on the table. There were all kinds of bottles on that table. Everyone seemed to enjoy this game.

Slowly, something began to happen. Their voices got louder and louder. I could hear that profanity had stopped by for a round of Tunk. It almost made me want to run under a table. What was going on? What could these bottles be doing? What was in these bottles that could have made these people so upset, so loud? Some people were leaning out of their chairs; others had fallen asleep. These bottles did all this; there was no way I would want to drink anything out of them. Some of the people drank straight from the bottles. Some poured the contents into a glass, while others poured into a cup with some ice—it didn't seem to matter how they poured. It all appeared to have the same effect. It all seemed to make them be something they were not. How could this have happened? How could this go on? Well, it must have been a plan. Must have been folks looking forward to these bottles. Everybody was happy when they got to the table. Nobody had a sad face in the room. They all got happy when they got to the table. They all welcomed these bottles. These colorful bottles. These odd-shaped bottles. But they had a magical way of changing the whole atmosphere. Now, we were kids just playing around, we didn't know anything about the game they were playing or what the contents of the bottles were, but we knew without a doubt, every time those bottles appeared on the table, all hell broke loose. We saw people who were quiet and docile come alive and awake, full of vigor and energy. I said to myself, "What in the world has happened here?" How in the world you could sleep as a child, knowing that all this commotion was going on in your house? It was terrible, absolutely terrible.

Alcohol is one of those things I remember seeing. I remember seeing my mother and others drink alcohol, and it was terrible. It was terribly scary at times, because they became so unpredictable. They could be laughing at one moment, then later crying. Worst, they could be crying one moment and then fighting. Music, dancing, and drinking were a part of my family culture at one time.

Did it ever seem to be a problem? I think it did, because I could not understand after all the fun and laughter how could it change to tears and frustration. What did those bottles do to them, especially my mother?

My mom was born and raised in Durham, North Carolina, in 1930. She moved to Baltimore as a teenager and stayed with her aunt and uncle. At age eighteen, she had her first child, and she would go on to have eight more. She was one of the strongest women I have ever met, because she was so determined to give the best to her children. But we all have a life challenge. Her challenge was alcohol.

I remember asking my mother several times not to drink as tears rolled down my face. I had to be around eight years old when I first made this request. I asked her many times not to drink, and I'm not sure what made her listen. I know she told me that she did not want me to see her that way as I grew up. She wanted to be a better example to my siblings and me.

I'm not sure when it happened, but she began to go to a church on Pennsylvania Avenue on the west side of Baltimore. The church was Christ Temple Church, and the pastor was Reverend Sylvester Waddy. She became a faithful usher at the church and took this little boy with her to morning service, and evening service too on Sundays. She had turned her life around. We call that type of cessation or stopping of drinking alcohol a "spontaneous remission."[1] It is a kind of recovery that does not require AA meetings, nor does it need any medications. It was just a decision she made, and the alcohol consumption ceased, and she began to utilize a spiritual program to manage her recovery from alcohol. Spontaneous remission is unexplainable. She never returned to drinking again in her life. She was in her forties when she made this decision.

Now, some might say I was the catalyst for this change, being that I was the youngest child. I'm not sure if I was the change agent, but I was a contributing agent. I am so grateful for the decision she made. Now, even though I grew up seeing this drinking of alcohol in my life, I was very curious about what it meant to be drunk. So, one day, I was hanging out with a group of my friends and decided this was going to be my day. It was around the Christmas holidays, and we always played a lot of cards, namely the game of Spades. It was probably eight of us who would get together at Dereck and Devery's home. They had the best parents in the world. To have Jeff, Angelo, Greg, Ty, Dramus, Adrian, and me down in the basement playing cards to the wee hours of the morning—they were the best. I think they were just happy we were not roaming the streets of Baltimore—at least they knew where we were. We were teenagers at the time.

On occasions, we would have some beer, and no one got out of control with their drinking—until this night. I was determined to see what it felt like being drunk. I was drinking Bacardi rum and beer while my friends played cards. I was on a quest to get drunk. The only thing I remember was drinking and drinking and then waking up on the sofa in the morning, my head down with an awful headache. I had no idea what had happened. I heard the washing machine running, and I said to my friend Adrian, "Why is the washing machine running?"

He said, "Be quiet, I don't want to hear from you. I'm about to bust you in your head because you vomited on my shoes, and my shoes are getting washed."

I was so embarrassed that I had done such a thing, but I had no recollection of my behavior. I apologized, but it didn't seem like he, Dereck, or Devery were happy with me.

Later that day, I caught up with Adrian. We were just walking and talking about my drunken behavior. He was telling me all the wild things I had done, and of course I denied it all. He exclaimed, "I got you on tape. I had you taped." Adrian had recorded me while I was in my state of drunkenness. I have learned since that what I endured was a "blackout."[2] When you have a sudden loss of short-term memory, and you are disinhibited, that's a blackout. You say things you should not say and will do things you should not do. I had blacked out from all that rapid drinking the evening before. I never gave my liver time to break down the alcohol before it could get to my brain. The liver recognizes alcohol as a poison.[3] The liver immediately tries to process it and break it down and get it out of the body. When one drinks alcohol too rapidly, the liver can't break it down, and therefore, alcohol will begin to go to the brain, and excessive alcohol to the brain can cause a problem.[3] One common problem is a blackout, or alcohol intoxication.[4] A temporary loss of short-term memory and disinhibition can mean trouble. You have nothing to stop you from what you want to say or do. There is a part of the brain that under normal circumstances prevents us from saying or doing certain things.[5] If we said or did everything that came to our minds, we would not feel safe or comfortable, and we could jeopardize the safety and comfort of others.

I had almost no inhibitions when asked about who I liked at Mergenthaler High School. I talked about this classmate I liked. I had no restraint, and so I was the center of entertainment as I was asked question after question. They asked me in the room what kind of things I would do to her, and I told them whatever they asked. I told them I would take her clothes off and what I would do to her body. I had no idea that children were in the room as I elaborated the details. I could hear laughing as they made a mockery of me, and I was totally unaware I was even doing this and I had no recall after this event.

Another shocker to me was my voice tone. I sounded like a demon. I thought my voice dragged on. I kept asking Adrian, "Who is this person on this tape?" It did not sound like me. I sounded like someone from the *Exorcist*. I didn't recognize that it was me talking. I kept saying, "Who was this? It doesn't sound like me," and Adrian said, "It is you, Joe," but the voice on the tape seemed demonic. It seemed like a demon spirit was speaking through my lips. Have you seen the *Exorcist* and all the other demon possession movies? I was like one of those characters. After listening to that tape, I was so embarrassed. I threw the tape into the nearby pool on the corner of Harford Avenue and Oliver Street in East Baltimore.

I would go on to drink again, but never did I ever get drunk again. I would have a beer when I got into my twenties, but I remember one time my mother saw me drinking at a cookout. She had such a look on her face of shock, and I told her, "It's just a beer." She was not happy about it, and I put it away and shortly after that I just made a decision that I didn't need a beer to fit in. Sometimes when you go to a gathering such as a cookout, club, or party, everyone else is drinking, and you don't want to be the odd person, and so you pick up a drink. You have this drink just to fit in, but I learned that I didn't have to do that anymore, and so I just totally ceased drinking in my early twenties. I didn't need any more casual drinking of any sort.

Alcohol has been a part of our culture for many years, but from 1920 to 1933 there was a constitutional ban on alcohol in the United States called Prohibition.⁶ In 1933 we as a country again legalized alcohol.⁶ There are all sorts of theories as to why we legalized it. Some say we were facing an enormous financial deficit called the Great Depression and America needed a revenue source, so we taxed alcohol. Others say Al Capone and his fellow gangsters were so bent on illegally selling it, in a constant battle with the law, that finally the profit needed to be removed from the underworld mobsters.

With the approval of alcohol, we brought about a crisis. The alcohol was relaxing and made people feel right. But the risk outweigh the benefits. Alcohol use is the third-most-common preventable death that occurs in America. (Number one most preventable is smoking, and second is obesity, which can lead to disease such as high blood pressure, heart attacks, and poor circulation).⁷

First, we should talk about the liver. The liver is the largest internal organ, weighing about three pounds. It is responsible for so many things, but one chief duty of the liver is to get toxins or poisons safely out of the body.⁸ Alcohol is considered a poison from the standpoint of the liver.⁹ Once alcohol is consumed, the liver breaks it down to make it safe to leave the body before it accumulates and makes you act all wacky like I did.³

Over time drinking too much alcohol, the liver gets damaged, as alcohol destroys the same organ that is responsible for getting rid of it.⁹ Damage to the liver takes place as a result of years of drinking, but it doesn't always happen to every drinker. Cirrhosis is simply a scarred liver.⁹ First, the liver was swollen and inflamed, and when it healed, it healed as scar tissue. The liver stops functioning properly, and we get backup fluids called ascites (*a-site-ees*), this may be what has happened when you see a large abdomen on a person. Ascites is more than a beer belly, folks. Ascites is fluid that has pooled in the belly as a result of liver damage.[10]

You may also see jaundice. Jaundice is the yellow coloring of the body, especially the eyes. Because the liver is not able to break down old red blood cells, which turn yellow after 120 days, the person looks yellow. In the bone marrow, red blood cells are produced, but after 120 days they lose their pigmentation or color, so the liver gets rid of them.[11] A damaged liver might not be able to do so. Thus, they float throughout the body.

Another body organ that gets affected by drinking is the pancreas. It is located right behind the liver, and it has two primary functions. One, it releases insulin, which helps us get the fuel for our body parts and helps with digesting starches we eat by releasing chemicals called enzymes.[12] Alcohol can damage the pancreas and make it inflamed too, just like the liver. Alcohol can cause the pancreas to eat away at itself, and this is known to be very painful. The person is hospitalized and given no foods by mouth until this organ heals.[12]

The answer to all these problems is simple. It is not all that complicated, the advice of the medical provider. It doesn't take a rocket scientist to figure this one out. The person has to STOP DRINKING and NEVER DRINK AGAIN. It sounds simple, but it can be the worst information an alcoholic could hear.

In my opinion, alcohol is one of the most harmful drugs that a person can place in their body. So why do people drink?

Well, how much time do you have? There are a lot of reasons why people drink alcohol. Some people grew up with drinking alcohol in their environment. Others might say, "I just experimented with it and took a liking to it." Some might even say, "I inherited it." Whatever the reason might be, one has to ask this question—does alcohol affect my functioning in life? Do I drink despite harm it causes me or others around me?

Ask yourself, when I drink, am I at risk of having an accident when I get in my car? Will I drive above the speed limit and run off the road and maybe kill myself? I won't try to tell you all the problems we have with alcohol in America; I will just give you some statistics from MADD, AKA (Mothers Against Drunk Driving)

EACH DAY, MORE THAN 300,000 PEOPLE DRIVE DRUNK, BUT ONLY ABOUT 3,200 ARE ARRESTED.[13]

OVER 40% OF ALL TENTH GRADERS DRINK ALCOHOL.[14]

IN 2013, 9.9 MILLION PEOPLE REPORTED DRIVING UNDER THE INFLUENCE OF ILLICIT DRUGS IN THE PAST YEAR.[15]

ALMOST HALF OF ALL DRIVERS WHO WERE KILLED IN CRASHES AND TESTED POSITIVE FOR DRUGS ALSO HAD ALCOHOL IN THEIR SYSTEM.[16]

ABOUT ONE-THIRD OF ALL DRIVERS ARRESTED OR CONVICTED OF DRUNK DRIVING ARE REPEAT OFFENDERS.[17]

OVER 1.1 MILLION DRIVERS WERE ARRESTED IN 2014 FOR DRIVING UNDER THE INFLUENCE OF ALCOHOL OR NARCOTICS.[18]

IN 2014, THREE TIMES AS MANY MALES WERE ARRESTED FOR DRUNK DRIVING AS FEMALES (401,904 VS. 130,480).[19]

THE RATE OF DRUNK DRIVING IS HIGHEST AMONG 26- TO 29-YEAR-OLDS (20.7%).[20]

IN FATAL CRASHES IN 2014, THE HIGHEST PERCENTAGE OF DRUNK DRIVERS WAS FOR DRIVERS AGES 21 TO 24 (30%), FOLLOWED BY AGES 25 TO 34 (29%) AND 35 TO 44 (24%).[21]

THE AVERAGE PERSON METABOLIZES ALCOHOL AT THE RATE OF ABOUT ONE DRINK PER HOUR.[22]

A STANDARD DRINK IS DEFINED AS 12 OUNCES OF BEER, 5 OUNCES OF WINE, OR 1.5 OUNCES OF DISTILLED SPIRITS, WHICH CONTAIN THE SAME AMOUNT OF ALCOHOL.[23]

IMPAIRMENT IS NOT DETERMINED BY THE TYPE OF DRINK, BUT RATHER BY THE AMOUNT OF ALCOHOL DRUNK OVER TIME.[24]

What can we do for the person who is drinking? You want to tell me, "I don't have a problem with drinking." We call that denial. Denial is the action of declaring something to be untrue.[25] The alcoholic first has to be made aware that there is a problem. There are several screening tools to help with this dilemma the person might be facing. One that I am familiar with is the CAGE assessment tool. The name *CAGE* is derived from the four questions of the tool: Cut down, Annoyed, Guilty, and Eye-opener.[26]

## CAGE Substance Abuse Screening Tool

Directions: Ask these four questions and use the scoring method described below to determine if drug addiction exists and needs to be addressed.

## CAGE Questions

1. Have you ever felt you should cut down on your drinking?
2. Have people annoyed you by criticizing your drinking?
3. Have you ever felt bad or guilty about your drinking?
4. Have you ever had a drink first thing in the morning to steady your nerves or to get rid of a hangover (eye-opener)?

## CAGE Questions Adapted to Include Drug Use (CAGE-AID)

1. Have you ever felt you ought to cut down on your drinking or drug use?
2. Have people annoyed you by criticizing your drinking or drug use?

3. Have you felt bad or guilty about your drinking or drug use?
4. Have you ever had a drink or used drugs first thing in the morning to steady your nerves or to get rid of a hangover (eye-opener)?

Scoring: Item responses on the CAGE questions are scored 0 for "no" and 1 for "yes" answers, with a higher score being an indication of alcohol problems. A total score of two or greater is considered clinically significant.

The typical cutoff for the CAGE is two positive answers. However, the Consensus Panel recommends that the primary care clinicians lower the threshold to one positive answer to cast a wider net and identify more patients who may have substance abuse disorders. Some other screening tools are available.

**CAGE Source: Ewing 1984**

Enough talk about the problem—how does an alcoholic get drug-free? That's what this book is all about, right? Yes, it is about getting drug-free. So this is for the person who is having a problem with alcohol, in that some area of their life is not functioning well. It could be at work, in relationships, or just within you. Whatever the dysfunction, you have decided you just need help. Now let's talk.

You can try stopping on your own, if you can handle the alcohol withdrawals you are about to face, starting with anxiety and sweating, then leading to tremors, possible seizures, and even death.[27] The brain looks for alcohol, and there is none, and now you experience agitation in the brain. Alcohol withdrawals can send you to the hospital or even kill you if not treated under medical care. You can progress to delirium tremens, also called DTs, which can occur a couple of days after your last drink. DTs are when you get confused. The blood pressure rises and the brain is headed for collapse and possibly death. You will need an intensive care unit admission at your local hospital. DTs can occur about two days after your last drink.[27]

Alcohol detox is very familiar and needed for a person with a history of drinking, and it is safe. During the detox, you will be given medications like Librium and Valium to calm the brain down. These medications mimic alcohol to the brain, but they safely allow the brain to get restored. The detox period can vary from a few days to a week or more. It all depends on your body.

Know that detox is not treatment. After you have successfully detoxed, you may be thinking of attending your local Alcoholic Anonymous meeting. You only have to have a desire not to drink to attend. In 1935, AA was developed by Bill Wilson and Dr. Bob Smith.[28] The group was formed to help persons struggling with drinking alcohol to find refuge. It continues to be a place of education and hope for the person struggling to get drug-free from alcohol. Look up Alcoholics Anonymous chapters at www.aa.org.

You could try to quit on your own, and some have, though I don't have the statistics. I believe it happens all the time. I don't see conquering addiction as mind over matter because I have learned the brain is altered by substances such as alcohol and drugs. However, some people have found the will to say no and never looked back. They have found something that was more important to them than drinking; for some, it was their relationships, their jobs, or just their peace of mind.

Some people find support in their faith. They trust in God to help them remain drug-free. I believe God can do anything except fail! Your belief in God can arrest and deliver you from the things that would try to destroy your life, such as alcoholism.

Further, along with your religion, AA, and your own will to change, medications can help with your recovery. The medications we use in the treatment of alcoholism are Antabuse, naltrexone, or Revia/Vivitrol and Campral.[29]

Antabuse is the brand name and disulfiram (*di-sul-fi-ram*) is the generic name. It is a pill that makes the alcoholic sick if they drink alcohol. The person takes it daily and must be twelve hours without alcohol before they can start receiving Antabuse or disulfiram. It works to make the person fearful to drink. The most common complaint I hear from patients taking Antabuse is that it makes them feel tired. If a person drinks alcohol while on Antabuse, they may have reactions that could be quite awful. The side effects of Antabuse are flushing, throbbing in head and neck, throbbing headache, respiratory difficulty, nausea, copious vomiting, sweating, thirst, chest pain, palpitation, dyspnea, hyperventilation, tachycardia, hypotension, syncope, marked uneasiness, weakness, vertigo, blurred vision, and confusion.[30] The liver must be monitored to make sure the medication does not damage it, but in my experience of giving the medication, I have never seen liver damage as a result of persons taking Antabuse (disulfiram)

I see Antabuse/disulfiram prescribed more than Revia/naltrexone or its (injectible version Vivitrol/naltrexone) or Campral/acamprosate. These latter two drugs work to reduce cravings for alcohol.[29] Revia is a once-a-day pill. Vivitrol is a monthly injection, and Campral is a three-times-a-day dose. [29]

There are many choices for the person struggling to overcome alcohol addiction. There is no one-stop shop to get drug-free. Maybe the family has pressured you to get sober or drug-free. Perhaps you are facing a loss of employment if you don't. When you can see that the benefits of being drug-free outweigh the risks of drinking, then you are moving in the right direction!

"What if I fail the first time I try?" You might ask. Addiction and recovery is like a roller coaster. It can be up and down, but don't get off the ride. It doesn't have to remain this way. Each time you fall is another opportunity to learn from that experience and do better the next time. Sometimes it takes years of battling with addiction, because there is a part of you that doesn't see why you have to stop. You can't understand how if something makes you feel so good it could be wrong. There is a battle raging in your head over whether it is wrong or right to do what you are doing. How have you violated your right to freedom? Freedom is the right to do whatever you want to do as long as you don't affect your rights or others. I'm sorry to have to tell you this, but you have violated your freedom! You put yourself and others at risk when you drink; that's why the family has left you, your job is about to let you go, and you are not happy living with yourself.

    Good news: there is a better life being drug-free. You can think better when you are not intoxicated. You can think straight now. You can wake up thinking about the possibilities and the potential you have in life. You have a chance to be all you want to be. Nothing is interfering with your brain. Nothing is slowing you down and causing your nerve connections not to work well. Come on, you deserve to be drug-free. You're too good to be addicted to alcohol because you are valuable!

## Chapter 4

1. What is Spontaneous Remission from Drug Addiction? (January 25, 2012). Retrieved March 21, 2016, from http://www.recoveryfirst.org/what-is-spontaneous-remission-from-drug-addiction/
2. Blackout. (2016). *The Free Dictionary* Retrieved March 21, 2016, from http://medical-dictionary.thefreedictionary.com/blackout
3. Lieber, C. S. (2000). Alcohol and the liver: metabolism of alcohol and its role in hepatic and extrahepatic diseases. *The Mount Sinai Journal of Medicine, New York*, 67(1), 84-94.
4. Alcohol Alert. (October 1998). Retrieved March 21, 2016, from http://pubs.niaaa.nih.gov/publications/aa42.htm
5. Iyer, S. (June 22, 2014). The Brain's Neurons Balance Excitement, Inhibition, In Order To Remain Healthy. Retrieved March 21, 2016, from http://www.medicaldaily.com/brains-neurons-balance-excitement-inhibition-order-remain-healthy-289338
6. Blocker Jr, J. S. (2006). Did prohibition really work? Alcohol prohibition as a public health innovation. *American journal of public health*, 96(2), 233-243.
7. The Most Preventable Causes of Death in the U.S. (2016). Retrieved March 21, 2016, from https://www.healthaliciousness.com/blog/The-Most-Preventable-Causes%20of%20Death-in-the-United-States.php

8. Kiernan, F. (1833). The anatomy and physiology of the liver. *Philosophical transactions of the Royal Society of London*, *123*, 711-770.
9. Bellentani, S., Saccoccio, G., Costa, G., Tiribelli, C., Manenti, F., Sodde, M., ... & Brandi, G. (1997). Drinking habits as cofactors of risk for alcohol induced liver damage. *Gut*, *41*(6), 845-850.
10. Nabili, S. (February 24, 2016). *Ascites*. Retrieved March 21, 2016, from http://www.medicinenet.com/ascites/article.htm
11. Herrine, S. (2016). *Jaundice in Adults*. Retrieved March 21, 2016, from http://www.merckmanuals.com/professional/hepatic-and-biliary-disorders/approach-to-the-patient-with-liver-disease/jaundice
12. Apte, M. Pirola, R and Wilson, J. (2016). *Pancreas: Alcoholic Pancreatitis It's All Alcohol, Stupid* Retrieved March 21, 2016, from http://www.medscape.com/viewarticle/706319
13. Arrest data: Federal Bureau of Investigation. "Crime in the United States: 2014." https://www.fbi.gov/about-us/cjis/ucr/crime-in-the-u.s/2014/crime-in-the-u.s.-2014/tables/table-29. Incidence data: Centers for Disease Control and Prevention. "Alcohol-Impaired Driving Among Adults — the United States, 2012." *Morbidity and Mortality Weekly Report.* August 7, 2015 / 64(30);814-817. http://www.cdc.gov/mmwr/preview/mmwrhtml/mm6430a2.htm
14. Miech, R. A., Johnston, L. D., O'Malley, P. M., Bachman, J. G., & Schulenberg, J. E. (2015). Monitoring

the Future national survey results on drug use, 1975-2014: Volume I, Secondary school students. Ann Arbor: Institute for Social Research, University of Michigan, pp. 599.
15. Substance Abuse and Mental Health Services Administration. Results from the 2013 National Survey on Drug Use and Health: Summary of National Findings. Rockville, MD: Substance Abuse and Mental Health Services Administration, 2014. http://www.samhsa.gov/data/sites/default/files/NSDUHresultsPDFWHTML2013/Web/NSDUHresults2013.pdf.
16. Johnston, L. D., O'Malley, P. M., Bachman, J. G., & Schulenberg, J. E. (2011). Monitoring the Future national survey results on drug use, 1975-2011. Volume I: Secondary school students (NIH Publication No. 10-7584). Bethesda, MD: National Institute on Drug Abuse, pp. 734.
17. Fell, Jim. "Repeat DWI Offenders in the United States." Washington, DC: National Department of Transportation, National Highway Traffic Safety Administration Traffic Tech No. 85, February 1995.
18. Federal Bureau of Investigation. "Crime in the United States: 2014." https://www.fbi.gov/about-us/cjis/ucr/crime-in-the-u.s/2014/crime-in-the-u.s.-2014/tables/table-29.
19. Federal Bureau of Investigation. "Crime in the United States: 2014." https://www.fbi.gov/about-us/cjis/

ucr/crime-in-the-u.s/2014/crime-in-the-u.s.-2014/tables/table-33.
20. Substance Abuse and Mental Health Services Administration. Results from the 2013 National Survey on Drug Use and Health: Summary of National Findings. Rockville, MD: Substance Abuse and Mental Health Services Administration, 2014. http://www.samhsa.gov/data/sites/default/files/NSDUHresultsPDFWHTML2013/Web/NSDUHresults2013.pdf.
21. National Highway Traffic Safety Administration. "Traffic Safety Facts 2014: Alcohol-Impaired Driving." Washington DC: National Highway Traffic Safety Administration, 2016. http://www-nrd.nhtsa.dot.gov/Pubs/812231.pdf.
22. Michigan State University. "Basic Alcohol Information." East Lansing, MI: Michigan State University, 2003.
23. National Highway Traffic Safety Administration. "Alcohol Screening and Brief Intervention in the Medical Setting." DOT HS 809 467. Washington, DC: National Highway Traffic Safety Administration, July 2002.
24. Insurance Institute for Highway Safety. "Q&A: Alcohol: General." Arlington, VA: National Highway Insurance Institute for Highway Safety, March 2012.
25. *Denial.* (2016). *Oxford Dictionary.com* Retrieved March 24, 2016, from http://www.bing.com/search?q=denial&src=IE-TopResult&FORM=IETR02&conversationid=

26. Cage Substance Abuse Screening Tool. Retrieved March 24, 2016, from http://www.hopkinsmedicine.org/johns_hopkins_healthcare/downloads/CAGE%20Substance%20Screening%20Tool.pdf
27. Alcohol Withdrawals. (February 2016). Retrieved March 24, 2016, from http://www.webmd.com/mental-health/addiction/alcohol-withdrawal-symptoms-treatments
28. History of Alcoholic Anonymous. Retrieved March 24, 2016, from http://www.the-alcoholism-guide.org/history-of-alcoholics-anonymous.html
29. Understanding Alcohol Abuse. (March 2015). *Webmd.com* Retrieved March 24, 2016, from http://www.webmd.com/mental-health/addiction/understanding-alcohol-abuse-treatment?page=2
30. Disulfiram. (2016). *Drugs.com* Retrieved March 24, 2016, from http://www.drugs.com/pro/disulfiram.html

# CHAPTER 5
# To the Family and Friends of Those Still Using

I feel for families of addicts. So much you don't know, and it's hard to separate yourself from this person you love, the person who has become addicted. You might want to blame yourself for the way they turned out—maybe there was something you didn't see that was going wrong, you're saying to yourself, and if only you had stopped it in time, this would not have happened.

Let me try to help you. First, it's not all your fault your loved ones have become alcoholics or drug addicts. There are a variety of reasons why people develop a liking for alcohol or drugs. Sometimes there is no known reason. We learn from our environments, whatever they might be.

My story was that I saw alcoholism as a child, and those experiences have never left my memory, but that was not all for me. I also had a group of friends who drank, and I was influenced on that front. I got the idea of what would it be like being drunk. My time around my friends made me curious about what it might feel like to be drunk or under the influence of alcohol. I wanted that experience and I sought after it. Make sure you read Chapter 4.

Sometimes, I believe, we want a change from our normal feelings to another way of feeling. For instance, my son asked me one day as a kindergarten student, "Dad, why do people drink alcohol?" I replied, "People want their minds to be changed, Goshen." I believe sometimes people really want their minds to be changed.

Some of your family members who are addicted might tell you they drink and use drugs to avoid the nasty withdrawals. They are correct, but it still is the same thing, because they too want a change. They want their physical symptoms or the way they feel to normalize and go back to the state in which they were under the influence of alcohol or drugs. They want to feel better and not have those darn withdrawals. No matter how they "slice it," they still are looking for a change. In this case, they just want to feel better.

Family and friends of the person using, I have watched how you bring them into treatment with the wish, "I just hope they will stop using alcohol or drugs." We in the field are hoping for the same thing. We want them to stop too, but it's going to cost them something. Your faces are filled with tears, anger, frustration, and disappointment because your question is a good one. When is enough enough—what will it take for them to go in the opposite direction?

Well, let's go through the process together. You have gotten your person to take the first step, to come for treatment.

They overcame their own resistance to do what you recommended. Maybe they were on the verge of being kicked out of the home, or maybe you were going to leave them, but they were given the final call. The ultimatum.

First day of treatment, they are sitting with you in the lobby, and you all are waiting for the assessor to call your names for you get them admitted and "fixed." "What is taking so long?" you say, and "When are you going to get called?" "How long do you have to wait for treatment?" also comes to your mind. Finally the call goes out: "Mr. or Mrs. Jones, I'm ready to meet with you," the assessment person says.

You all come into my office, and you are scared. "What kind of place is this?" you are saying to yourself. It is an outpatient substance abuse clinic. You've never had to do this before. The assessment person asks the person you brought into treatment if they would prefer to have you there or would rather meet alone. For the most part, the assessor will meet with the person alone. Think about it—talk about an embarrassing moment. There will be a lot of gathering of history of the person's alcohol and drug use.

It still amazes you that you could have been fooled and bamboozled. How did this person fool you when you care so much about them? How come you didn't see the signs? I have heard several stories of how men and women tricked family and friends into believing they didn't have a problem with alcohol or drugs. Some of those family and friends were left with a loss of money, disappointments, embarrassments, and little hope in those who were using.

But they are here now in the treatment center—maybe under duress, but nevertheless, they are here. You agree to step out, and the assessment person is very friendly but firm with the person trying to give it a try. They start out with "What brings you to treatment today?" Then there are more questions:

> How old were you when you first used drugs or alcohol?
> How much money do you spend on alcohol or drugs?
> What have been some of the consequences of drinking or using drugs?
> Has your use interfered with your relationships, wife, siblings, children, friends?
> Has your use interfered with work, hobbies?
> Do you use more than you intended to?

These are just a few of the questions during their assessment. The goal is to determine if there is an addiction. We want to know if alcohol or drugs has caused the person to continue to use, despite the harm to themselves or others around them. Once the assessment person has determined that this person has met criteria for treatment, then treatment can begin now that they are diagnosed with an alcohol or substance use disorder. It can be alcohol, Heroin, Cocaine, marijuana, or any other drug.

This person has done a heroic act, and you should be proud of them, but now what? Your loved one will be assigned to a professional counselor to help them reach the goal of abstinence from alcohol or drugs. There can be no more drinking or drugging. The primary purpose for a person in drug treatment is to stop drinking or using drugs. The primary goal of treatment is not to get a job or to get back with their children or apply for social services or even social security to file for disability. The number-one goal is not to drink or use drugs. I know I'm being redundant, but that needs to be very clear. Urines and breathalyzer readings need to be negative. That's the primary goal.

So the person's counselor will help them get drug free and remain drug free. They will provide your loved one with information to help them accept that they have an addiction, because sometimes people are in denial. They don't believe they are alcoholics or drug addicts or substance users. They don't see themselves the way other people see them. A few great talents in our world never got a chance to see themselves the way others saw them, as drug-free individuals, and they went to their graves early as a result of denial. Denial means the inability to see that something is wrong with the way you are living your life despite all the clues in front of you. All the people around you see the problem, but despite all the warnings and information people try to convey to you, you don't see it the same way they do.

Moreover, this person who is using will have the most important person in their life assigned to them, and that's their counselor in this process of recovery. They will need to surrender their way of doing things to a person who holds the keys to their future of a life without alcohol or drugs. They may have been a "skilled" alcoholic or drug user, but they lack skill when it comes to ways to abstain from use. I know this for a fact, because if they had the skills, they would not have been assigned a counselor—they would have no need for substance-abuse treatment.

Now comes the hard part: they get the plan of how to abstain from drug use from their counselor. They have thought it over, and everybody is waiting to see if they will do it to the best of their ability. Sometimes some extra support is needed in addition to the counselor, like housing and medications.

First, let's talk about housing. A program for housing is very useful when it comes to your loved one; it gives them a place in another environment away from what is normal for them. Your loved one can have a significant degree of comfort, because where they used to live put them in danger due to a drugging and drinking environment.

Some outpatient programs are set up for the person to take part in a house environment. There are some long-term programs, for example in our city of Baltimore, which allow your loved ones to have housing along with treatment. Housing allows this person to be in an environment with others like them who are striving for the goal of being drug free. Unfortunately, sometimes a person in the house may revert to using alcohol or drugs, and that will be addressed, as it threatens the safety of all in the house. The person may be given a chance to stay in the house but follow a strict set of rules to maintain sobriety, or they may be asked to leave if they are selling drugs. A stern set of rules might include going to more Alcoholics Anonymous (AA) or Narcotics Anonymous (NA) meetings or having more sessions with their counselor.

It could be a combination of things to get the person to abstain from the use of alcohol or drugs.

There's more. If in despite of having a counselor to help your person who has been using, they still have cravings to use, that's when medications are called in. Many believe addiction is a disease and it develops in the brain after the introduction of alcohol or drugs, so it would be right to treat this disease with medications. I talk about the medications for treating alcohol, opioid, and Cocaine addiction and the assistance of a medical team of providers in chapters 2, 3 and 4.

We have to do everything we can to not have this person who once used alcohol or drugs start using again. This person is too valuable. It's not going to be easy, but we who do the work of addiction treatment are up for the challenge!

Stress should be at a low, and it is already stressful just to come in for treatment. They will need some time to work on this addiction. They will not be able to do or return to the activities you expect of them for several months while they work on ways to abstain from drinking or drugging—activities like being a full-time spouse or parent. They will need some time to concentrate on their recovery.

Sometimes your loved one will want to use while in treatment. Sometimes a substance user will become angry or stressed in treatment, and they will make a comment like "You're going to make me go out." When they say something like this, they probably mean you're going to cause them to go out and use again. Why can't it cause them to do something positive, instead of something negative? I believe the event should instead cause them to go into a meeting or a support group, or to go to a telephone and call a sober friend, or to go to church.

My point is, stress can cause us to pull on the things that help us be strong. Their coping skills used to be to go get a drink or use drugs, but they will now learn new coping skills to deal with life stresses in healthy ways. Drinking and drugging again is not an option!

That's a lot about the person who is using; let's talk about you, the person whose loved one is in treatment. You still don't quite understand this alcoholism and drug addiction stuff. You have good willpower, and nothing overtakes you or causes you to use alcohol or drugs. I applaud you for being so in control, but might I suggest you take the time to learn more about what your loved one might be going through by electing to go to meetings that will help you understand addiction. Al-Anon (www.al-anon.org) runs meetings for those who are family members and friends of people with alcoholism, and Nar-Anon (www.nar-anon.org) runs meetings for family members and friends of people with substance-abuse addictions other than alcohol. Al-Anon and Nar-Anon are support groups that can help you to understand more about drug addiction. They are an excellent way to assist you, along with the counselor, in being a support to the person with the substance-use disorder, and all that you will gain will better help your family member or friend be able to approach treatment and be successful, because you will be more understanding and compassionate.

As their nurse, I will do all I can to educate your loved one about addiction and how it affects their mental and physical health. I promise to be honest, caring, and knowledgeable. I want to gain their trust and your trust. I want what you want, and that is for your loved one to be alcohol and drug free. I realize without a doubt that they are valuable and that they are worth more than a life of being an alcoholic (person with an alcohol use disorder) or addicted to drugs (person with a substance use disorder).

# CHAPTER 6

# Other Drugs

I have said all I wanted to say in this book about drug addiction to Heroin, Cocaine and alcohol. This chapter contains fact sheets about four other commonly abused drugs according to the Drug Enforcement Agency: Marijuana, K-2 "Spice", Ecstasy (MDMA), and Methamphetamine (Meth). Feel free to make copies of these pages, as they don't require my permission.

**Drug Enforcement Administration •**
For more information, visit *www.dea.gov*

Marijuana **Overview:** Marijuana is a mind-altering (psychoactive) drug, produced by the Cannabis sativa plant. Marijuana contains over 400 chemicals. THC (delta-9-tetrahydrocannabinol) is believed to be the main chemical ingredient that produces the psychoactive effect.

**Street names:** Aunt Mary, BC Bud, Blunts, Boom, Chronic, Dope, Gangster, Ganja, Grass, Hash, Herb, Hydro,

Indo, Joint, Kif, Mary Jane, Mota, Pot, Reefer, Sinsemilla, Skunk, Smoke, Weed, Yerba

**Looks like:** Marijuana is a dry, shredded green/brown mix of flowers, stems, seeds, and leaves from the Cannabis sativa plant. The mixture typically is green, brown, or gray in color and may resemble tobacco.

**Methods of abuse:** Marijuana is usually smoked as a cigarette (called a joint) or in a pipe or bong. It is also smoked in blunts, which are cigars that have been emptied of tobacco and refilled with marijuana, sometimes in combination with another drug. Marijuana is also mixed with foods or brewed as a tea.

**Effect on mind:** When marijuana is smoked, the THC passes from the lungs and into the bloodstream, which carries the chemical to the organs throughout the body, including the brain. In the brain, the THC connects to specific sites called cannabinoid receptors on nerve cells and influences the activity of those cells. Many of these receptors are found in the parts of the brain that influence pleasure, memory, thought, concentration, sensory and time perception, and coordinated movement. The short-term effects of marijuana include problems with memory and learning, distorted perception, difficulty in thinking and problem-solving, and loss of coordination. The effect of marijuana on perception and coordination are responsible for serious impairments in driving abilities. Long-term chronic marijuana use is associated with Amotivational Syndrome, characterized by apathy, impairment of judgment, memory and concentration, and loss of motivation, ambition and interest in the pursuit of personal goals. High doses of marijuana can result in mental confusion, panic reactions and hallucinations. Researchers have also found an association between marijuana use and an increased risk of depression; an increased risk and earlier onset of schizophrenia and other psychotic disorders, especially for teens that have a genetic predisposition.

**Effect on body:** Short-term physical effects from marijuana use may include sedation, blood shot eyes, increased heart rate, coughing from lung irritation, increased appetite, and decreased blood pressure. Like tobacco smokers, marijuana smokers experience serious health problems such as bronchitis, emphysema, and bronchial asthma. Extended use may cause suppression of the immune system. Because marijuana contains toxins and carcinogens, marijuana smokers increase their risk of cancer of the head, neck, lungs and respiratory track. Withdrawal from chronic use of high doses of marijuana causes physical signs including headache, shakiness, sweating, stomach pains and nausea, as well as behavioral signs including restlessness, irritability, sleep difficulties and decreased appetite.

**Drugs causing similar effects:** Hashish and hashish oil are drugs made from the cannabis plant that are like marijuana, only stronger. Hashish (hash) consists of the THC - rich resinous material of the cannabis plant, which is collected, dried, and then compressed into a variety of forms, such as balls, cakes, or cookie like sheets. Pieces are then broken off, placed in pipes or mixed with tobacco and placed in pipes or cigarettes, or smoked. The main sources of hashish are the

Middle East, North Africa, Pakistan and Afghanistan. Hashish Oil (hash oil, liquid hash, cannabis oil) is produced by extracting the cannabinoids from the plant material with a solvent. The color and odor of the extract will vary, depending on the solvent used. A drop or two of this liquid on a cigarette is equal to a single marijuana joint. Like marijuana, hashish and hashish oil are both Schedule I drugs.

**Overdose effects:** No death from overdose of marijuana has been reported.

**Legal status in the United States:** Marijuana is a Schedule I substance under the Controlled Substances Act. Schedule I drugs are classified as having a high potential for abuse, no currently accepted medical use in treatment in the United States, and a lack of accepted safety for use of the drug or other substance under medical supervision. Marinol, a synthetic version of THC, the active ingredient found in the marijuana plant, can be prescribed for the control of nausea and vomiting caused by chemotherapeutic agents used in the treatment of cancer and to stimulate appetite in AIDS patients. Marinol is a Schedule III substance under the Controlled Substances Act. Schedule III drugs are classified as having less potential for abuse than the drugs or substances in Schedules I and II, and have a currently accepted medical use in treatment in the U.S., and abuse of the drug may lead to moderate or low physical dependence or psychological dependence.

**Common places of origin:** Marijuana is grown in the United States, Canada, Mexico, South America and Asia. It can be cultivated in both outdoor and in indoor settings.

**Drug Enforcement Administration** •
For more information, visit *www.dea.gov*

K2 or Spice **Overview:** K2 or "Spice" is a mixture of herbs and spices that is typically sprayed with a synthetic compound chemically similar to THC, the psychoactive ingredients in marijuana. The chemical compounds typically include HU-210, HU-211, JWH-018, and JWH-073. K2 is commonly purchased in head shops, tobacco shops, various retail outlets, and over the Internet. It is often marketed as incense or "fake weed." Purchasing over the Internet can be dangerous because it is not usually known where the products come from or what amount of chemical is on the organic material.

**Street names:** Bilss, Black Mamba, Bombay Blue, Fake Weed, Genie, Spice, Zohai **Looks like** K2 is typically sold in small, silvery plastic bags of dried leaves and marketed as incense that can be smoked. It is said to resemble potpourri.

**Methods of abuse:** K2 products are usually smoked in joints or pipes, but some users make it into a tea.

**Effect on mind:** Psychological effects are similar to those of marijuana and include paranoia, panic attacks, and giddiness.

**Effect on body:** Physiological effects of K2 include increased heart rate and increase of blood pressure. It appears to be stored in the body for long periods of time, and therefore the long-term effects on humans are not fully known.

**Drugs causing similar effects:** Marijuana

**Overdose effects** There have been no reported deaths by overdose.

**Legal status in the United States:** On Tuesday, March 1, 2011, DEA published a final order in the Federal Register temporarily placing five synthetic cannabinoids into Schedule I of the CSA. The order became effective on March 1, 2011. The substances placed into Schedule I are 1-pentyl-3-(1-naphthoyl) indole (JWH-018), 1-butyl-3-(1-naphthoyl) indole (JWH-073), 1-[2-(4-morpholinyl) ethyl]-3-(1-naphthoyl)indole (JWH-200), 5-(1,1-dimethylheptyl)-2-[(1R,3S)-3-hydroxycyclohexyl]-phenol (CP-47,497), and 5-(1,1-dimethyloctyl)-2-[(1R,3S)-3-hydroxycyclohexyl]-phenol (cannabicyclohexanol; CP-47,497 C8 homologue). This action is based on a finding by the Administrator that the placement of these synthetic cannabinoids into Schedule I of the CSA is necessary to avoid an imminent hazard to the public safety. As a result of this order, the full effect of the CSA and its implementing regulations including criminal, civil and administrative penalties, sanctions, and regulatory controls of Schedule I substances will be imposed on the manufacture, distribution, possession, importation, and exportation of these synthetic cannabinoids.

**Common places of origin:** Manufacturers of this product are not regulated and are often unknown since these products are purchased via the Internet whether wholesale or retail. Several websites that sell the product are based in China. Some products may contain an herb called damiana, which is native to Central America, Mexico, and the Caribbean.

**Drugs causing similar effects:** Marijuana

**Drug Enforcement Administration •**
For more information, visit *www.dea.gov*

Ecstasy or MDMA **Overview:** MDMA acts as both a stimulant and psychedelic, producing an energizing effect, distortions in time and perception, and enhanced enjoyment of tactile experiences. Adolescents and young adults use it to reduce inhibitions and to promote: euphoria, feelings of closeness, empathy, and sexuality. Although MDMA is known among users as Ecstasy, researchers have determined that many Ecstasy tablets contain not only MDMA but also a number of other drugs or drug combinations that can be harmful, such as: methamphetamine, ketamine, Cocaine, the over-the-counter cough suppressant dextromethorphan (DXM), the diet drug ephedrine, and caffeine. In addition, other drugs similar to MDMA, such as MDA or PMA, are often sold as Ecstasy, which can lead to overdose and death when the user takes additional doses to obtain the desired effect.

**Street names:** Adam, Beans, Clarity, Disco Biscuit, E, Ecstasy, Eve, Go, Hug Drug, Lover's Speed, MDMA, Peace, STP, X, XTC

**Looks like:** MDMA is mainly distributed in tablet form. MDMA tablets are sold with logos, creating brand names for users to seek out. The colorful pills are often hidden among colorful candies. MDMA is also distributed in capsules, powder, and liquid forms.

**Methods of abuse:** MDMA use mainly involves swallowing tablets (50-150 mg), which are sometimes crushed and snorted, occasionally smoked but rarely injected. MDMA is also available as a powder. MDMA abusers usually take MDMA by "stacking" (taking three or more tablets at once) or by "piggy-backing" (taking a series of tablets over a short period of time). One trend among young adults is "candy flipping," which is the co-abuse of MDMA and LSD. MDMA is considered a "party drug." As with many other drugs of abuse, MDMA is rarely used alone. It is common for users to mix MDMA with other substances, such as alcohol and marijuana.

**Effect on mind:** MDMA mainly affects brain cells that use the chemical serotonin to communicate with each other. Serotonin helps to regulate mood, aggression, sexual activity, sleep, and sensitivity to pain. Clinical studies suggest that MDMA may increase the risk of long-term, perhaps permanent, problems with memory and learning. MDMA causes changes in perception, including euphoria and increased sensitivity to touch, energy, sensual and sexual arousal, need to be touched, and need for stimulation. Some unwanted psychological effects include: confusion, anxiety, depression, paranoia, sleep problems, and drug craving. All these effects usually occur within 30 to 45 minutes of swallowing the drug and usually last 4 to 6 hours, but they may occur or last weeks after ingestion.

**Effect on body:** Users of MDMA experience many of the same effects and face many of the same risks as users of other stimulants such as Cocaine and amphetamines. These include increased motor activity, alertness, heart rate, and blood pressure. Some unwanted physical effects include: muscle tension, tremors, involuntary teeth clenching, muscle cramps, nausea, faintness, chills, sweating, and blurred vision.

High doses of MDMA can interfere with the ability to regulate body temperature, resulting in a sharp increase in body temperature (hyperthermia), leading to liver, kidney and cardiovascular failure. Severe dehydration can result from the combination of the drug's effects and the crowded and hot-conditions in which the drug is often taken. Studies suggest chronic use of MDMA can produce damage to the serotonin system. It is ironic that a drug that is taken to increase pleasure may cause damage that reduces a person's ability to feel pleasure.

**Drugs causing similar effects:** No one other drug is quite like MDMA, but MDMA produces both amphetamine-like stimulation and mild mescaline-like hallucinations.

**Overdose effects:** In high doses, MDMA can interfere with the body's ability to regulate temperature. On occasions, this can lead to a sharp increase in body temperature (hyperthermia), resulting in liver, kidney, and cardiovascular system failure, and death. Because MDMA can interfere with its own metabolism (that is, its break down within the body), potentially harmful levels can be reached by repeated drug use within short intervals.

**Legal status in the United States:** MDMA is a Schedule I drug under the Controlled Substances Act, meaning it has a high potential for abuse, no currently accepted medical use in treatment in the United States, and a lack of accepted safety for use under medical supervision.

**Common places of origin:** MDMA is a synthetic chemical made in labs. Seized MDMA in the U.S. is primarily manufactured in, and smuggled across our borders from, clandestine laboratories in Canada and, to a lesser extent, the Netherlands. A small number of MDMA clandestine laboratories have also been identified operating in the U.S.

**Drug Enforcement Administration** •
For more information, visit *www.dea.gov*

Methamphetamine **Overview:** Methamphetamine (meth) is a stimulant. The FDA-approvedbrand-name medication is Desoxyn®.

**Street names:** Batu, Bikers Coffee, Black Beauties, Chalk, Chicken Feed, Crank, Crystal, Glass, Go-Fast, Hiropon, Ice, Meth, Methlies Quick, Poor Man's Cocaine, Shabu, Shards, Speed, Stove Top, Tina, Trash, Tweak, Uppers, Ventana, Vidrio, Yaba, Yellow Bam

**Looks like:** Regular meth is a pill or powder. Crystal meth resembles glass fragments or shiny blue-white"rocks" of various sizes.

**Methods of abuse:** Meth is swallowed, snorted, injected, or smoked. To intensify the effects, users may take higher doses of the drug, take it more frequently, or change their method of intake. In some cases, meth abusers go without food and sleep whiletaking part in a form of binging known as a "run." Meth users on a "run" inject as much as a gram of the drug every two to three hours over several days until they run out of meth or become too disorganized to continue.

**Effect on mind:** Meth is a highly addictive drug with potent central nervous system (CNS) stimulant properties. Those who smoke or inject it report a brief, intense sensation, or rush. Oral ingestion or snorting produces a long-lasting high instead of a rush, which reportedly can continue for as long as half a day. Both the rush and the high are believed to result from the release of very high levels of the neurotransmitter dopamine into areas of the brain that regulate feelings of pleasure. Long-term meth use results in many damaging effects, including addiction. Chronic meth abusers exhibit violent behavior, anxiety, confusion, insomnia, and psychotic features, including paranoia, aggression, visual and auditory hallucinations, mood disturbances, and delusions —such as the sensation of insects creeping on or under the skin. Such paranoia can result in homicidal or suicidal thoughts. Researchers have reported that as much as 50% of the dopamine-producing cells in the brain can be damaged after prolonged exposure to relatively low levels of meth. Researchers also have found that serotonin-containing nerve cells may be damaged even more extensively.

**Effect on body:** Taking even small amounts of meth can result in increased wakefulness, increased physical activity, decreased appetite, rapid breathing and heart rate, irregular heartbeat, increased blood pressure, and hyperthermia (overheating).High doses can elevate body temperature to dangerous, sometimes lethal, levels as well as cause convulsions and even cardiovascular collapse and death. Meth abuse may also cause extreme anorexia, memory loss, and severe dental problems.

**Drugs causing similar effects:** Cocaine and potent stimulant pharmaceuticals, such as amphetamines and methylphenidate, produce similar effects.

**Overdose effects:** High doses may result in death from stroke, heart attack, or multiple organ problems caused by overheating.

**Legal status in the United States:** Methamphetamine is a Schedule II stimulant under the Controlled Substances Act, which means that it has a high potential for abuse and limited medical use. It is available only through a prescription that cannot be refilled. Today there is only one legal meth product, Desoxyn®. It is currently marketed in 5-milligram tablets and has very limited use in the treatment of obesity and attention deficit hyperactivity disorder (ADHD).

**Common places of origin:** Mexican drug trafficking organizations have become the primary manufacturers and distributors of methamphetamine to cities throughout the United States, including in Hawaii. Domestic clandestine laboratory operators also produce and distribute meth but usually on a smaller scale. The methods used depend on the availability of precursor chemicals. Currently, meth is mainly made with diverted products that contain pseudoephedrine. The Combat Methamphetamine Epidemic Act of 2005 requires retailers of non-prescription products containing pseudoephedrine, ephedrine, or phenylpropanolamine to place these products behind the counter or in a locked cabinet. Consumers must show identification and sign a logbook for each purchase.

## CHAPTER 7
# Overdose Death Statistics

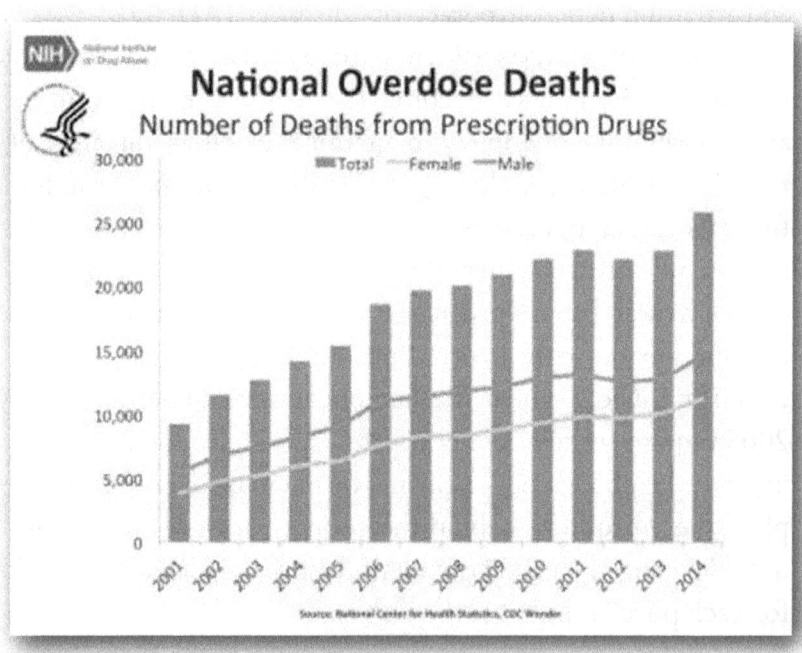

National Overdose Deaths—Number of Deaths from Prescription Drugs. The figure above is a bar chart showing the total number of U.S. overdose deaths involving prescription drugs from 2001 to 2014. The chart is overlayed by a line graph showing the number of deaths by females and males. From 2001 to 2014 there was a 2.8-fold increase in the total number of deaths.

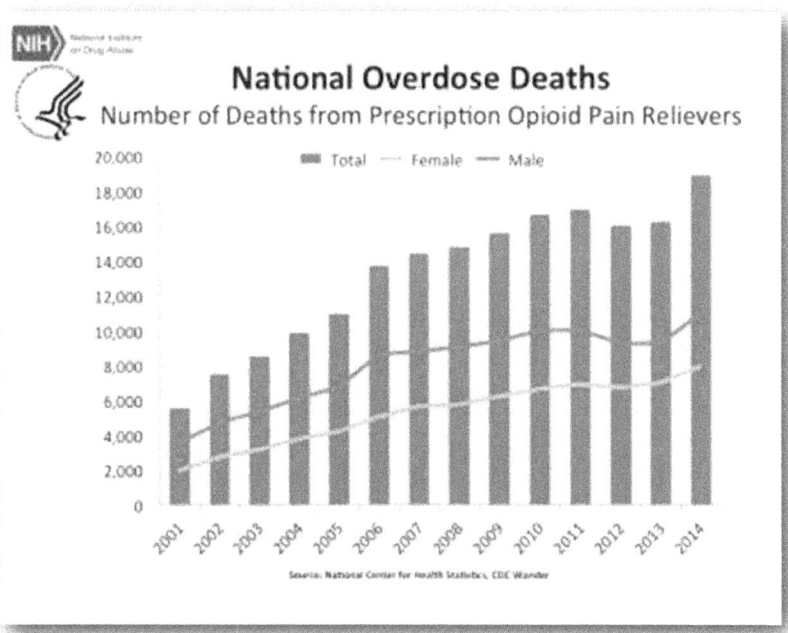

National Overdose Deaths—Number of Deaths from Prescription Opioid Pain Relievers. The figure above is a bar chart showing the total number of U.S. overdose deaths involving opioid pain relievers from 2001 to 2014. The chart is overlayed by a line graph showing the number of deaths by females and males. From 2001 to 2014 there was a 3.4-fold increase in the total number of deaths.

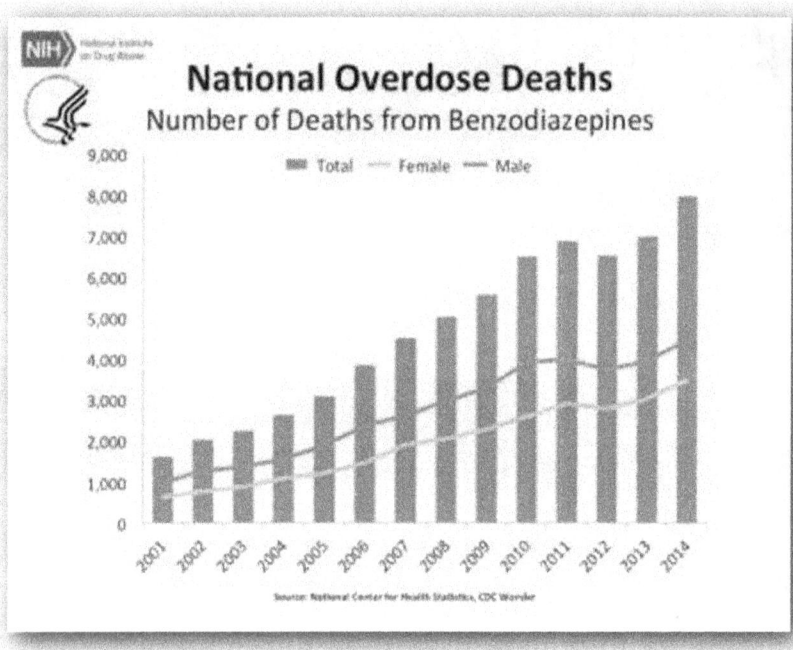

National Overdose Deaths—Number of Deaths from Benzodiazepines. The figure above is a bar chart showing the total number of U.S. overdose deaths involving benzodiazepines from 2001 to 2014. The chart is overlayed by a line graph showing the number of deaths by females and males. From 2001 to 2014 there was a 5-fold increase in the total number of deaths.

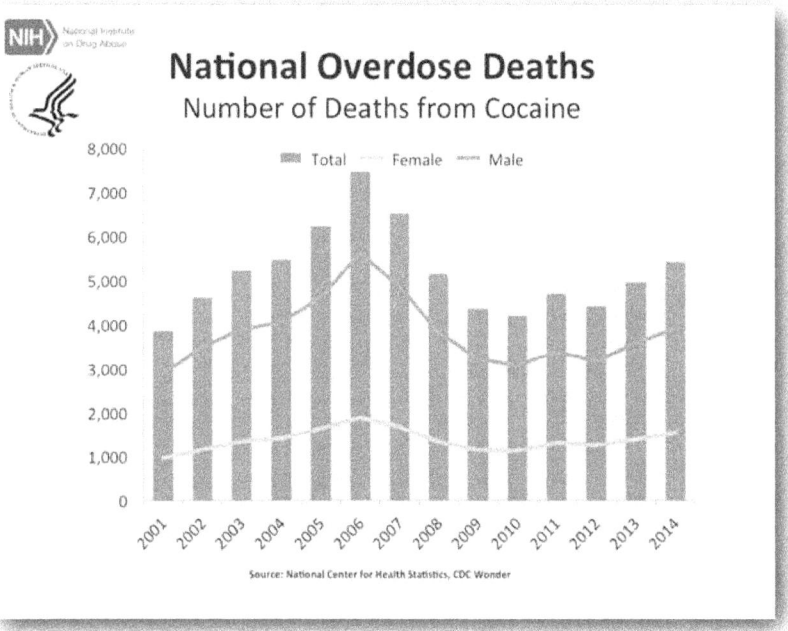

National Overdose Deaths—Number of Deaths from Cocaine. The figure above is a bar chart showing the total number of U.S. overdose deaths involving cocaine from 2001 to 2014. The chart is overlayed by a line graph showing the number of deaths by females and males. From 2001 to 2014 there was a 42 percent increase in the total number of deaths.

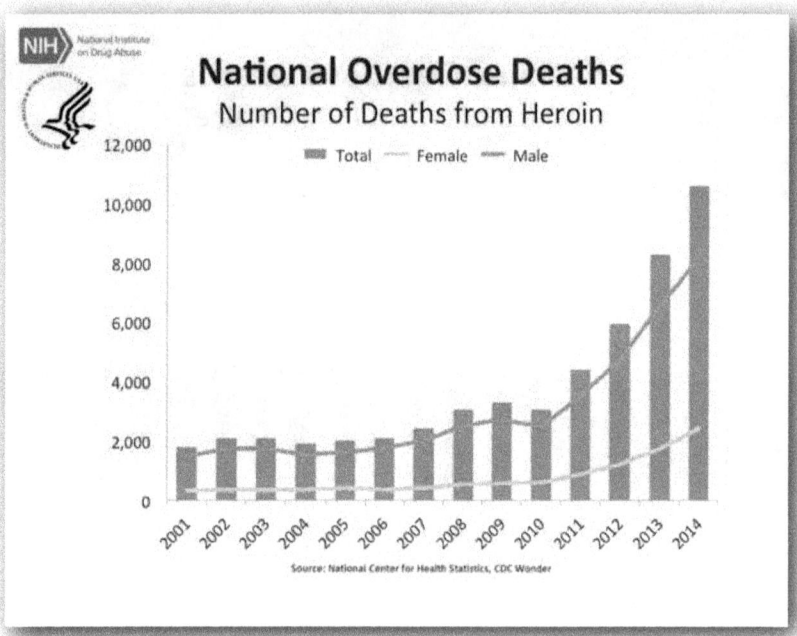

National Overdose Deaths—Number of Deaths from Heroin. The figure above is a bar chart showing the total number of U.S. overdose deaths involving heroin from 2001 to 2014. The chart is overlayed by a line graph showing the number of deaths by females and males. From 2001 to 2014 there was a 6-fold increase in the total number of deaths.

www.ingramcontent.com/pod-product-compliance
Lightning Source LLC
Chambersburg PA
CBHW071305040426
42444CB00009B/1875